BEST OF | QUINOA

Rena Patten's

BEST OF | QUINOA

ENJOY THE BEST OF RENA'S MOST-LOVED QUINOA RECIPES

Contents

WHAT IS QUINOA?

(PRONOUNCED KEEN-WAH)

You may be asking what exactly is quinoa? Quinoa, pronounced 'keen-wah', is a tiny little grain, but not just any grain. It is a grain that is considered to be almost a complete food, being very high in protein, full of vitamins, totally gluten-, wheat- and cholesterol-free, usually organic and of absolutely great benefit to everyone's diet. It is very easy to prepare and tastes absolutely delicious.

In a nutshell, quinoa is a complete source of protein and has all the essential amino acids, trace elements and vitamins you need to survive.

It is an ancient seed native to the Andes Mountains in South America. It has been around for over 5,000 years and is known to have been a staple food of the ancient civilization of the Incas having sustained them for centuries.

It was used to supplement their diet of potatoes and corn. It was commonly referred to as the 'mother grain' or 'gold of the Incas' and was considered sacred. It is still considered a very important food in the South American kitchens. I have always referred to quinoa as the Supergrain of the Century.

As stated earlier, although most commonly referred to as a grain, quinoa is in actual fact a seed. It is the seed of a leafy plant called Chenopodium quinoa of the Chenopodium/Goosefoot plant family and is distantly related to the spinach plant. I like to refer to it as a grain because to me it gives people a rough idea about the size of this grain, whereas the term 'seed' could imply that it is similar in size to the seed in a citrus fruit or an olive or an avocado for instance.

Quinoa is a pure and complete grain and almost the perfect food as the degree of nutrition in each tiny grain is regarded as being quite potent. It has the highest amount of protein of any grain and this unusually high amount of protein is actually a complete protein containing all nine essential amino acids, the only grain to contain all nine essential amino acids. The quality of this protein has been likened, by the World Health Authority, as being the closest to milk.

The amino acid composition is extremely well balanced and has a particularly high content of the amino acid lysine which is essential in our diet for tissue repair and growth. Quinoa is a must for vegans and vegetarians who may be concerned about the level of protein in their daily diet.

It is also a very good source of manganese, magnesium, potassium, phosphorous, copper, zinc, vitamin E, vitamin B6, riboflavin, niacin and thiamine. It has more calcium than cow's milk, is an excellent antioxidant, is rich in dietary fibre and has more iron than any other grain. It also has the highest content of unsaturated fats and a lower ratio of carbohydrates than any other grain plus a low glycemic index (GI) level. The health benefits to be gained from using this grain are truly enormous.

Quinoa has a huge range of uses and lends itself beautifully to so many dishes. When cooked it has a very delicate texture and is lovely in soups, sweets, makes wonderful salads, pasta, breads, and delicious vegetarian and non-vegetarian meals. You can also make pastry for pies using quinoa flour—bear in mind though that pastry made with quinoa flour may go a little soggy quicker than if you were using normal gluten flour. I consider quinoa to be a perfect food for coeliac sufferers, vegans and vegetarians.

My philosophy in food has always been that people with special dietary requirements should not miss out and should be able to enjoy most of the food that people without special dietary requirements enjoy. Now with quinoa and knowledge of the many different ways that it can be prepared, people can do just that!

I think of and use quinoa as a special natural food, nature's very own superfood. It is very easy to prepare, easy to digest and most enjoyable to eat. It is very light on the stomach and you don't tend to feel at all heavy after eating a meal made with quinoa. I also find certain sweets prepared with the quinoa flour can be lighter than those prepared with normal wheat flour.

To those who are gluten- and wheat-intolerant, quinoa is a food that can offer you a greater variety of ideas for your everyday table and for those special meals that you can offer your guests.

WHAT DOES QUINOA LOOK LIKE?

The grain itself is tiny and round with a fine band around it ending in what looks like a minute 'tail'. As it cooks the 'tail' spirals out and almost detaches itself. It becomes very distinct from the rest of the grain in the shape of an outer white ring that is clearly visible. When cooked the grain becomes very soft in the centre while the 'tail' retains a bit of crunch giving it a texture all of its own. When the grain is cooked it has a very delicate texture and it expands to almost four times its original volume.

There are many different varieties of quinoa and it is available in grain form, flakes and flour, making it suitable for cooking in many different ways. The color of the grain can vary from white (opaque) or pale yellow to red, purple, brown and black. The recipes in this book extensively use the grain, flake or flour form of this wonderful grain in one way or another so as to show you just how easy it is to use this supergrain in so many different ways.

It is available at most health food stores and in the health food section of the larger supermarkets. Some shops also stock quinoa milk; it is however quite expensive and not that readily available. Toasted quinoa is also available but why not make your own. You can keep a jar of it in your pantry to sprinkle on your porridge, ice cream or use instead of croutons in your soups or sprinkled over your salads for added crunch. Homemade toasted quinoa tends to keep for quite a while stored in a glass jar with a tight-fitting lid. You can also buy puffed quinoa.

HOW TO PREPARE QUINOA

Quinoa grows in arid climates, at high altitudes and very poor soil. It is suggested that the survival of this plant over the centuries could be attributed to a soapy-like substance called 'saponin', which creates a bitter coating on the grain and protects it from the harsh, high-altitude weather as well as any birds or insects.

This bitter soapy coating must be removed before cooking. Although most grain comes pre-washed and ready to cook. It is still a good idea to rinse it thoroughly before use to remove any residue of 'saponin'. I always tell people that they must rinse the grain before cooking.

Simply place the quinoa into a fine sieve and rinse under cold running water. After thoroughly wetting the quinoa, rub it lightly between your fingertips, drain well and it is ready to cook. Make sure that you do use a very fine sieve as the grains are so tiny and will otherwise go straight through a standard colander or strainer.

Quinoa cooks very quickly simmered in water, stock, juice or milk. One part quinoa, two parts liquid and 10 minutes in the saucepan are usually all that is needed to prepare quinoa as a basic cooked grain. However, you may need to cook the quinoa a little longer if the liquid is denser than water, such as a sauce, stock or milk. And also the darker grains, the red and black varieties, take a little longer to cook and tend to retain a little bit more of a crunch. The length of the cooking time can also vary depending on the brand and age of the grain. Resting the cooked quinoa covered, for 10–15 minutes after cooking, will ensure it is softer and fluffier. Use a fork to fluff up the quinoa after it has been cooked.

Quinoa can be cooked in the microwave, although this is not my preferred method—I find it a bit too fiddly and it seems to take longer. To cook quinoa in the microwave place 1 part quinoa to 2 parts liquid in a microwave-proof dish and cook on high for 7 minutes; stir, then cover with plastic wrap and stand for 7–8 minutes. Depending on your microwave you may need to vary the cooking time. You can also cook quinoa in a rice cooker in the same way that you would on the stove top. One part quinoa to two parts water cooked on the rice setting then rest, covered, for 5–10 minutes.

For an added nutty taste, you can toast the quinoa before cooking. Rinse and drain the quinoa well, then dry roast in a small non-stick frying pan. When the grains start to pop, remove the pan from heat and transfer the quinoa to a saucepan with 2 parts liquid, bring to the boil, then reduce the heat and simmer, covered, for 10 minutes.

You can also sprout quinoa by placing 1 part rinsed quinoa with 3 parts water in a jar with a lid and soak for about 2 hours; drain and rinse, then return to the jar with the lid on and leave to sprout. You must rinse them at least twice per day. They are very tiny sprouts and should be ready in about 2–3 days but must be eaten immediately as they do not last. You can use the sprouts in salads.

To prepare the salads from this book you will need to cook the quinoa first, cool completely and then combine with the other ingredients.

I make a lot salads using quinoa so I tend to cook a large batch of the grain and leave it in the refrigerator to use as I need it. Quinoa cooked in water will keep in the refrigerator for up to a week. For most of the other recipes in this book where the grain is used, the grain is actually cooked with the other ingredients, making them one-pot meals. Which colored grain you wish to use in your cooking is totally up to you. I have specified a color in only a few recipes and that was done purely for visual appeal.

Cooking appliances: It is important to remember that all cooking appliances, especially ovens, vary in their cooking time so you may need to experiment with your own to work out the correct cooking time.

Also cooking time can vary depending on the grain used, temperature of your cooking appliance and, believe it or not, even the type and size of saucepan used.

For the one-pot meals I find the best utensil to use is a large deep wide-surfaced frying pan with a lid. It not only holds a large quantity of ingredients but it also distributes and cooks the quinoa with all the other ingredients more evenly over a larger cooking surface.

Breakfast

CRUNCHY BREAKFAST MIX

Makes approx. 2.5kg

This is one of those mixes that is good to have on hand as it is not only great for breakfast. You can grab a handful of this at anytime. Good in school or work lunches. If you don't have maple syrup you can use golden syrup instead. Keep an eye on it while it is in the oven as it can burn easily. I have used the red quinoa in this recipe purely for the added crunch that you get from the darker grain.

Ingredients

- *140 g (5 oz) red quinoa, rinsed and drained*
- *350 ml (12 fl oz) water*
- *120 g (4½ oz) quinoa flakes*
- *125 g (4 oz) whole blanched almonds*
- *75 g (2½ oz) pepitas/pumpkin seeds*
- *75 g (2½ oz) sunflower seeds*
- *60 g (2 oz) sesame seeds*
- *2 tsps ground cinnamon*
- *½ tsp ground nutmeg*
- *1 tbsp vanilla*
- *110 g (4 oz) maple syrup*
- *70 g (3 oz) light brown sugar, tightly packed*
- *70 g (3 oz) honey*
- *2 tbsps vegetable or extra light olive oil*
- *150 g (5 oz) golden raisins*
- *125 g (4 oz) dried cranberries*

Method

Place quinoa into a small saucepan with the water. Bring to the boil, reduce the heat and simmer for 10 minutes until all the water is absorbed. Remove from the heat, uncover and cool completely.

Preheat oven to 160°C (325°F) and line two large baking trays with non-stick baking parchment/paper.

In a large bowl, mix together the quinoa flakes, cooled quinoa grain, almonds, pepitas, sunflower and sesame seeds, cinnamon and nutmeg.

Add the vanilla, maple syrup, brown sugar, honey and oil and mix really well, as you want all the ingredients to be completely coated.

Spread the mixture out evenly over the two trays in a single layer and bake for about 30–40 minutes until crisp and crunchy and a rich golden color. Stir once or twice through the baking time making sure you keep the mix evenly distributed in the tray.

Remove from the oven and cool, then stir in the raisins and cranberries and store in an airtight container when completely cold. Serve with milk or yogurt or sprinkle over porridge.

BREAKFAST BARS

Makes 16

These bars are great for breakfast on the run or for a quick but satisfying and nourishing snack. Pack them into school and work lunch boxes, take them to picnics or have them as an after-sport snack.

Ingredients

- *90 g (3½ oz) quinoa flour*
- *1 tsp gluten-free baking powder*
- *80 g (3 oz) quinoa flakes*
- *1 tsp ground cinnamon*
- *150 g (5 oz) brown sugar*
- *125 g (4 oz) dried cranberries*
- *125 g (4 oz) dried apricots, chopped*
- *90 g (3 oz) golden raisins*
- *125 g (4 oz) sunflower seeds*
- *60 g (2 oz) slivered almonds, chopped*
- *60 g (2 oz) butter*
- *110 g (4 oz) honey*
- *1 tsp vanilla bean paste*
- *2 extra large eggs, lightly beaten*

Preheat the oven to 180°C (350°F) and lightly grease a 29 x19 cm (12 x 7 ½ in) slice tin then line with baking paper. Greasing the tin first helps the paper stay in place.

Sift the flour and baking powder into a large bowl then stir in the quinoa flakes, cinnamon and sugar. Mix well, making sure you break up any lumps in the sugar.

Add the cranberries, apricots, raisins, sunflower seeds and almonds, mix well to combine.

Place butter and honey into a small saucepan and stir over low heat until butter has melted, and then stir in the vanilla.

Pour the melted butter and the eggs over the flour and fruit mixture and mix really well pressing the mixture together so it is well combined and not dry.

Using the back of a spoon, press mixture firmly into the prepared tin then bake for about 20–25 minutes until golden.

Remove from the oven and leave to cool in the tin for about 15 minutes and then cut into desired sized bars. Leave to cool in the tin for a little longer then carefully remove the slice with the paper and place on a cooling rack to cool completely.

BUTTERMILK BREAD LOAF

Makes 1 loaf

This is quite a dense bread and quick to make. It's not a conventional bread dough, but is more like a cake mixture. Everything is mixed together, poured into the tin and baked without having to wait for the dough to rise.

Ingredients

- *vegetable oil*
- *120 g (4½ oz) quinoa flakes, plus extra for loaf tin*
- *250 g (9 oz) quinoa flour*
- *1½ tsp baking soda (bicarbonate of soda)*
- *4 tsp brown sugar*
- *1½ tsp salt*
- *350 ml (12 fl oz) buttermilk*
- *2 eggs*
- *60 ml (2 fl oz) water*
- *½–1 tsp red or black quinoa grain*

Method

Preheat the oven to 190°C (375°F). Brush a 22 x 15 x 8 cm (8½ x 6 x 3 in) loaf tin with vegetable oil.

Combine the flour, baking soda, sugar and salt in a bowl, then mix in the 120 g (4½ oz) quinoa flakes. Whisk together the buttermilk, egg and water and slowly incorporate into the dry ingredients, mixing well. This will be a fairly wet mixture.

Pour the bread mixture into the prepared tin, sprinkle the top with quinoa grain and bake for about 60–70 minutes, until the bread is cooked, is deep golden and sounds hollow when tapped.

CREAMY APPLE AND CINNAMON PORRIDGE

Serves 4–6

You can make this with full or reduced fat milk or replace with any lactose-free milk.

Ingredients

- *2 apples*
- *240 ml (8 fl oz) water*
- *2–3 tbsps brown sugar*
- *80 g (3 oz) quinoa flakes*
- *700 ml (24 fl oz) milk*
- *1 tsp vanilla extract*
- *½–1 tsp ground cinnamon*

Coarsely grate the apples, keeping the skin on, and place into a medium-sized saucepan with the water and sugar. Bring to the boil then reduce the heat and simmer for 5 minutes to soften the apples.

Add the quinoa flakes, milk, vanilla and cinnamon to the saucepan and stir well. Start off with the lower amount of cinnamon and sugar, and increase according to taste.

Bring to the boil on medium heat. Once boiling, reduce the heat to low and simmer for about 5–7 minutes until the porridge is thick and creamy.

Serve with extra milk if needed and a good sprinkle of toasted quinoa (see recipe page 27).

FRUIT SMOOTHIES

Serves 1–2

Ingredients

- *100 g (3½ oz) frozen berries*
- *30 g (1½ oz) quinoa flakes*
- *1–2 tbsps honey*
- *240 ml (8 fl oz) low-fat milk*
- *60 ml (2 fl oz) water*
- *1 tsp vanilla extract*

Method

Place all the ingredients into a blender and blend until thick and smooth. For added protein, add an egg white. You can use apple juice instead of the milk or a bit of both. You can replace the frozen berries for other fruit such as bananas, mango and peaches or any fruit that can be placed in the freezer to have on hand and throw into a smoothie.

THE SUPER GREEN DRINK

Serves 1–2

Ingredients

- *2 handfuls fresh kale, washed and chopped*
- *1 large green apple, left unpeeled, remove the core and seeds*
- *40 g (1½ oz) quinoa flakes*
- *2 tbsps honey or agave syrup*
- *480 ml (16 fl oz) apple juice*
- *2 celery stalks, roughly chopped*
- *Small handful of fresh basil*
- *Juice ½–1 lemon*
- *2 tbsps natural Greek yogurt (optional)*
- *Ice cubes*

Method

Blend together all the ingredients until thick and smooth. If too thick, add a little water. You can vary the green leaves used according to your taste, you could use spinach and cucumber instead of the kale. Yogurt adds a little creamy richness to the drink; however, it tastes just as good without it.

MINI BANANA MUFFINS

Makes 48 mini muffins

These muffins are great for school lunches. This recipe makes a lot of mini muffins but they freeze really well. Just pop a frozen one in their school lunches. They are lovely eaten warm or cold and will remain fresh and moist for three to four days—kids love them.

Ingredients

- *2 over ripe bananas*
- *2 tsps lemon juice*
- *250 g (9 oz) quinoa flour*
- *190 g (6½ oz) superfine (caster) sugar*
- *1 level tsp baking soda (bicarbonate of soda)*
- *½ level tsp gluten-free baking powder*
- *½ tsp salt*
- *175 ml (6 fl oz) milk*
- *2 large eggs*
- *2 tsps vanilla paste or extract*
- *60 ml (2 fl oz) vegetable or extra light olive oil*
- *1 banana, for garnish (optional)*

Method

Preheat oven to 170°C (335°F) and line two 24-cup mini muffin tins with paper cases.

Mash the bananas with the lemon juice and set aside.

Sift together the flour, sugar, baking soda, baking powder and salt into a large bowl. Pour milk into a jug then lightly beat in the eggs, vanilla and oil.

Make a well in the centre of the dry ingredients and slowly pour in the liquid ingredients, mixing as you go until all the ingredients are combined.

Gently fold in the bananas; do not over mix.

Spoon the mixture into the prepared muffin tin, filling each case fairly close to the top and cover with a thin slice of banana, if using.

Bake for about 20 minutes until they have risen, are golden and firm to the touch, and a skewer comes out clean when tested.

SAVORY BUTTERMILK PANCAKES

Serves 4

For a vegetarian option, you can omit the ham and replace with finely chopped spinach or cooked corn kernels.

Ingredients

- *185 g (6½ oz) quinoa flour*
- *1 tsp baking powder*
- *1 tsp baking soda (bicarbonate of soda)*
- *salt and freshly cracked black pepper*
- *3 extra large eggs*
- *1 tbsp English mustard*
- *415 ml (14 fl oz) buttermilk*
- *200 g (7 oz) ham, chopped*
- *250 g (9 oz) ricotta cheese*
- *3 tbsps parmesan cheese, grated*
- *2 tbsps chopped fresh chives*
- *butter, for cooking*
- *maple syrup (optional)*

Sift together the quinoa flour, baking powder and baking soda then stir in the salt and pepper.

Whisk together the eggs and mustard, then mix in the milk.

Using a whisk, mix together the dry ingredients with the wet ingredients until you have a lump-free smooth batter, then stir in the ham, ricotta and parmesan cheeses and the chives. If possible, leave the batter to rest for at least 10 minutes. Heat a little butter in a non-stick pan on medium heat until it starts to bubble, pour about 75 ml (2½ fl oz) of the pancake mixture into the pan and lightly spread to form a circle.

Cook until bubbles form on the top of the pancake then gently flip over and cook on the other side for about 30 seconds.

Remove from pan and repeat with the remaining batter.

Serve pancakes hot with a drizzle of maple syrup.

RICOTTA PANCAKES WITH A BERRY SAUCE

Serves 4

You can use whatever other berries you prefer. Alternatively if you don't want to make a sauce you can stir 250 g (9 oz) of your favorite berry into the batter before cooking and serve with a drizzle of maple syrup.

Ingredients

- *185 g (6½ oz) quinoa flour*
- *1 tsp baking powder*
- *1 tsp baking soda (bicarbonate of soda)*
- *2 tbsps sugar*
- *3 extra large eggs*
- *1½ tsp vanilla bean paste or extract*
- *415 ml (14 fl oz) buttermilk*
- *400 g (14 oz) ricotta cheese*
- *butter, for cooking*
- *maple syrup (optional)*

BERRY SAUCE

- *500 g (17½ oz) frozen blueberries or berries of your choice*
- *50 g (2 oz) granulated sugar*

Method

Sift together the quinoa flour, baking powder and baking soda, then stir in the sugar.

Whisk together the eggs and vanilla, then mix in the buttermilk.

Using a whisk, mix together the dry ingredients with the wet ingredients until you have a lump-free, smooth batter, then stir in the ricotta cheese. Heat a little butter in a non-stick pan on medium heat until it starts to bubble, pour in about 75 ml (2½ fl oz) of the pancake mixture into the pan and lightly spread into a circle. Cook until bubbles form on the top of the pancake then gently flip over and cook on the other side for about 30 seconds.

Remove from pan and repeat with the remaining batter.

Serve pancakes stacked on top of one another with the berry sauce or alternatively you can serve them with a drizzle of maple syrup and, if you like, some natural yogurt.

To make the Berry Sauce: place frozen berries in a medium saucepan with the sugar and stir over a low heat. Once the berries have defrosted and sugar has melted and the mixture starts to bubble, gently simmer for about 2–3 minutes. Avoid stirring the berries: just lightly toss the pan every now and then.

You may need to vary the amount of sugar used depending on the tartness of the berries and your personal taste.

TOASTED QUINOA

Makes about 370 g (12½ oz)

This is really great to have in your pantry to use on or over just about anything you like. You can sprinkle it over your porridge, ice cream, stewed fruit, fruit salad, over soups in place of bread croutons or as a crunchy topping over salads.

Ingredients

- *185 g (6 oz) quinoa, rinsed and drained*
- *480 ml (16 fl oz) water*

Method

Place quinoa into a small saucepan with the water. Bring to the boil, reduce the heat, cover and simmer for 10 minutes until all the water is absorbed. Take off the heat and leave covered for 10 minutes.

Remove from the pan and spread out onto a baking tray and leave to cool completely. This is to remove as much moisture as possible.

When the quinoa has cooled, heat a large non-stick frying pan until fairly hot on medium-high heat. You will need a frying pan that has a large surface cooking area.

Spread the quinoa in the pan and dry-roast until you get a lovely crunchy and golden quinoa. This will take about 15–20 minutes and you will need to toss the quinoa in the pan regularly.

You will notice it starting to take on some color after about 8–10 minutes and it is at that point that you want to keep an eye on it as once it starts to toast the process doesn't take very long.

Alternatively, you can toast the quinoa in the oven. Preheat the oven to 200°C (400°F) and once the quinoa has cooled after boiling, spread on to a baking tray that has been lined with non-stick baking parchment/paper and bake, stirring regularly, for about 10–15 minutes until you reach the level of toastiness that you like. I prefer the stove-top method as I have more control over the cooking process; however, the end result is the same. Remove the toasted quinoa from the frying pan or the oven and allow to cool completely then store in a glass jar with a tight lid. It will keep in the jar for some time.

Soups

CREAMY COCONUT SEAFOOD SOUP

Serves 6

For convenience, I usually use a bought fresh marinara mix, which includes shelled shrimp, calamari, mussels and fish. You may want to remove the curry leaves before serving the soup.

Ingredients

- *4 cloves garlic*
- *1–2 long red chilies*
- *2 tbsp chopped fresh ginger*
- *1 tbsp ground turmeric*
- *1 tsp garam masala*
- *3 tbsp vegetable oil*
- *2 tsp mustard seeds*
- *1 tsp cumin seeds*
- *2 medium red onions, chopped*
- *good handful of fresh curry leaves*
- *2 x 400 g (14 oz) cans of coconut cream*
- *950 ml (32 fl oz) hot water*
- *pinch of saffron*
- *140 g (5 oz) quinoa grain, rinsed and drained*
- *1 kg (2 lb 3 oz) seafood marinara mix*
- *zest of 1 lime*
- *10 g (½ oz) cilantro (coriander) leaves*
- *sliced red chilies for serving*
- *fresh lime juice for serving*

Method

In a mortar and pestle, pound the garlic, chilies and ginger until a fine paste is formed. Stir in the turmeric and garam masala. Set aside.

Heat the oil in a large saucepan, add the mustard and cumin seeds and cook until they start to pop. Add the onion and cook on low to medium heat for about 5 minutes until soft. Stir in the curry leaves and the garlic and ginger paste and cook for a few seconds. Pour in the coconut cream, water and saffron, bring to the boil, reduce the heat and simmer, covered, for 20 minutes.

Add the quinoa to the soup. Simmer for 5 minutes. Add the seafood and lime zest, bring back to the boil and simmer, covered, on low heat for a further 10–15 minutes.

Stir in the fresh cilantro and serve with slices of chilies and a squeeze of lime juice.

BEETROOT, GINGER AND GARLIC SOUP

Serves 6–8

Black quinoa takes longer to cook than the other varieties so you will have to vary the cooking time according to how tender you would prefer the quinoa to be. You can use whichever quinoa you prefer: I used the black one only because I love the contrast of the black against the vibrant red of the beetroot. Don't forget to wear gloves when peeling the beetroot or you may end up with bright red hands.

Ingredients

- *1 tbsp extra virgin olive oil*
- *2 red onions, chopped*
- *4 large cloves garlic, chopped*
- *1 small knob ginger, grated to make about 1–2 tbsps*
- *1 kg (2 lb 4 oz) fresh beetroot, peeled and chopped*
- *few sprigs fresh thyme*
- *zest of 1 lime*
- *pinch of ground cloves*
- *2 litres (4½ pints) hot chicken or vegetable stock*
- *salt and freshly cracked pepper*
- *125 g (4½ oz) black quinoa, rinsed and drained*
- *lime juice, to serve*
- *natural Greek yogurt or sour cream, to serve*

Heat the oil in a large saucepan and sauté the onions until soft.

Add the garlic and ginger and cook for about 1–2 minutes until fragrant. Add the beetroot, thyme, lime zest and cloves and cook for another 2 minutes.

Pour in the stock and season with salt and pepper. Bring to the boil then reduce the heat and simmer for about 40–45 minutes until the beetroot is tender.

Puree the soup, bring back to the boil then add the quinoa, reduce the heat and simmer on low heat, covered for about 20–25 minutes until the quinoa is cooked. Serve garnished with a good squeeze of lime juice and a dollop of yogurt or sour cream.

ROASTED TOMATO AND FENNEL SOUP WITH BASIL AND GARLIC PESTO

Serves 6–8

This is one of my favorite soups and is absolutely delicious.

Ingredients

- *1.5 kg (3 lb 4 oz) firm, ripe tomatoes*
- *1 tsp sugar*
- *1 large fennel bulb*
- *2 onions, peeled*
- *1 head garlic, sliced in half*
- *extra virgin olive oil*
- *salt and freshly ground black pepper*
- *950 ml (32 fl oz) hot chicken or vegetable stock*
- *80 g (3 oz) red quinoa grain, rinsed and drained*

PESTO

- *2 cloves garlic*
- *4 tbsp extra virgin olive oil*
- *1 large handful fresh basil leaves*

Preheat the oven to 190°C (375°F).

Cut the tomatoes into quarters, place in a deep baking dish and sprinkle with the sugar. Cut the fennel and onions in half, then slice and place together on a baking tray with the unpeeled garlic. Drizzle the vegetables with extra virgin olive oil, season with salt and pepper and place in the oven to roast. The fennel and onions will take about 30–40 minutes and the tomatoes 45–55 minutes.

Once cooked, remove the skins from the tomatoes and squeeze the garlic out of its skin; discard the skins. Puree all the vegetables, then place in a saucepan with the stock and bring to the boil.

When the soup begins to boil add the quinoa grain, reduce the heat, cover, and cook on low heat for 15–20 minutes. Meanwhile, make the pesto by blending all the ingredients together.

Remove the soup from the heat and stir in the pesto. Adjust the seasoning and serve with a drizzle of extra virgin olive oil. Alternatively, you can serve the soup as is with a dollop of pesto.

CARROT, GINGER, GARLIC AND CILANTRO SOUP

Serves 4–6

This is a fairly thick soup and a meal on its own—if you prefer a thinner consistency, add extra hot water once cooking is finished.

Ingredients

- *1 tbsp cilantro (coriander) seeds*
- *2 tbsp olive oil*
- *1 large onion, chopped*
- *4 cloves garlic, chopped*
- *2 tbsp chopped fresh ginger*
- *1 kg (2 lb 3 oz) carrots, peeled and thickly sliced*
- *1½ litres (3 pints) hot vegetable stock*
- *salt and pepper to taste*
- *80 g (3 oz) uncooked quinoa grain*
- *240 ml (8 fl oz) hot water*
- *20 g (¾ oz) chopped fresh cilantro (coriander)*
- *fresh lime juice*

Method

Dry-roast the cilantro seeds in a small non-stick frying pan for about a minute until fragrant. Remove from heat and pound into a powder in a mortar and pestle; set aside.

Heat the oil in a large saucepan and cook the onion until soft. Add the garlic, ginger and ground cilantro seeds, and cook for 1 minute. Add the carrots, stock, salt and pepper, bring back to the boil and simmer covered for 40–50 minutes, until the carrots are tender.

Place the quinoa in a fine sieve, rinse under cold running water and drain.

Puree the soup, return to the saucepan and add the quinoa and hot water. Bring back to the boil, reduce heat, cover and simmer for 10 minutes

Stir in the fresh cilantro and simmer for 5–7 minutes more. Serve with a squeeze of lime juice.

CHORIZO SAUSAGE, BEAN AND CABBAGE SOUP

Serves 6–8

This is a thick and hearty soup perfect for those cold wintery nights. You can substitute the chorizo sausage with bacon or chicken. Or leave out the meat all together.

Ingredients

- *1 tbsp extra virgin olive oil*
- *3 chorizo sausages, diced*
- *2 red onions, finely chopped*
- *1–2 cloves garlic, finely chopped*
- *2 tsp sweet paprika*
- *1.3 kg (3 lb) Savoy cabbage, very finely shredded*
- *2 litres (4½ pints) hot chicken or veg stock*
- *2 bay leaves*
- *salt and pepper*
- *140 g (5 oz) quinoa, rinsed and drained*
- *2 x 400 g (14 oz) cans of cannellini beans, rinsed and drained*
- *3 tbsp fresh chives, chopped*

Method

Heat oil in a large saucepan and sauté the chorizo sausage and onions until onion is soft and chorizo golden. Stir in the garlic and paprika and cook for about 30 seconds.

Add the cabbage, stock and bay leaves and season with salt and pepper. Bring to the boil, reduce heat, cover and simmer for about 15 minutes.

Stir in the quinoa and continue simmering covered for another 15 minutes.

Add the beans and bring back to the boil. Reduce the heat, cover and simmer for 12–15 minutes until quinoa is cooked

Remove the bay leaf, stir in the chives, adjust the seasoning and serve.

CREAMY MUSHROOM SOUP

Serves 4–6

Keep in mind that quinoa will continue to expand a little more after cooking. If you find that your soup is too thick for your liking just thin down with extra water or stock.

Ingredients

- *2 tbsp olive oil*
- *1 large onion, chopped*
- *1 kg (2 lb 4 oz) mushrooms, sliced*
- *2 cloves garlic, chopped*
- *20 g (¾ oz) flat-leaf parsley, chopped*
- *salt and freshly cracked pepper*
- *1½ litres (3 pints) hot chicken stock*
- *90 g (3½ oz) quinoa, rinsed and drained*
- *120 ml (4 fl oz) cream*
- *parsley, chopped, for garnish*

Heat oil in a large saucepan and sauté onion until soft and golden.

Add the mushrooms and garlic and cook until mushrooms have collapsed.

Stir in the parsley, season with salt and pepper and cook on medium heat for 1–2 minutes.

Pour in the chicken stock and bring to the boil. Reduce heat and simmer for 20 minutes.

Remove from the heat and purée soup with either a stick blender or a food processor. Meanwhile, rinse and drain quinoa.

Place soup back on the stove, bring to the boil and stir in quinoa, reduce heat and simmer, covered, for 15–20 minutes.

Serve garnished with a drizzle of cream and chopped parsley.

LENTIL SOUP

Serves 6–8

Ingredients

- *400 g (14 oz) red lentils*
- *2 tomatoes, quartered*
- *1 large onion, chopped*
- *2 cloves garlic, chopped*
- *1 bay leaf*
- *1 tbsp olive oil*
- *salt and pepper to taste*
- *2 litres (4½ pints) water*
- *90 g (3½ oz) quinoa grain, rinsed*

GARNISH

- *60 ml (2 fl oz) olive oil*
- *1 medium onion, finely grated*
- *4 cloves garlic, finely grated*
- *3 tsp ground cumin*
- *extra virgin olive oil for serving*
- *lemon juice for serving*
- *red chili for serving*

Pick over lentils and remove any small stones and grit. Rinse under cold running water in a fine sieve until the water runs clear and drain.

Place the lentils in a large saucepan with the tomatoes, onion, garlic, bay leaf, olive oil, salt and pepper and 1.8 litres (4 pints) of water. Bring to the boil, reduce the heat, cover, and simmer on low for 30–40 minutes, until the lentils are tender and the soup has thickened. Skim off any foam that appears on the surface during the cooking.

Meanwhile cook the quinoa. Place it in a small saucepan with the remaining water. Bring to the boil, reduce the heat and simmer, covered, for 10 minutes. Remove from the heat and set aside.

When the lentils are cooked, take the pan from the heat and remove the tomato skins and bay leaf. Puree until smooth.

To prepare the garnish, heat the oil in a frying pan and sauté the onion and garlic until a deep golden color. Stir in the cumin, cook for 30 seconds, then stir in the cooked quinoa, mix well and check seasoning.

Place soup back on the heat, stir in quinoa mixture, mix well and heat through before serving with a drizzle of extra virgin olive oil, a squeeze of lemon juice and sliced fresh chilies.

ASIAN-STYLE SOUP

Serves 4

This one of those 'feel good' soups. It feels very cleansing and you feel good when eating it and actually feel it is doing you good. This one of my favorite soups and so quick to make. You can either make this soup simply as is or if you prefer you can add some finely sliced fresh raw chicken to the stock at the start. I always make a double quantity.

Ingredients

- *2 litres (4½ pints) chicken/vegetable stock*
- *1 stalk lemongrass, bruised*
- *2 star anise*
- *1 tbsp grated fresh ginger*
- *1 large clove garlic, peeled and lightly smashed*
- *125 g (4½ oz) quinoa grain, rinsed and drained*
- *90 g (3 oz) fresh shiitake mushrooms, sliced*
- *1 small bunch choy sum or bok choy (pak choy), washed well and cut into strips, chopped*
- *4 scallions (spring onions), sliced*
- *1 red chili, sliced*
- *2 tbsps fish sauce*
- *2–3 tbsps tamari soy sauce*
- *240 ml (8 fl oz) water or stock, extra*
- *Fresh bean sprouts, for garnish*
- *Fresh cilantro (coriander) leaves, garnish*
- *Lime juice, to taste*

Method

Bring the stock to the boil in a large saucepan with the lemongrass, star anise, ginger and garlic.

Add the quinoa, reduce the heat, cover and simmer on low heat for about 15 minutes until the quinoa is almost cooked.

Add the mushrooms, choi sum, scallions, chili, fish sauce and soy sauce, bring back to the boil, reduce the heat and simmer for another 5 minutes. Add an extra 240 ml (8 fl oz) of stock or water if you feel at this stage that the soup may be too thick.

Remove the lemongrass and serve garnished with bean sprouts, fresh cilantro leaves and lime juice.

SHRIMP AND CORN CHOWDER

Serves 6–8

For added richness and thickness, stir in some cream just before taking the soup off the heat.

Ingredients

- *2 tbsps extra virgin olive oil*
- *1 large onion, chopped*
- *2 cloves garlic, finely chopped*
- *2 x 400 g (14 oz) tinned creamed sweet corn*
- *500 g (17½ oz) frozen sweet corn kernels*
- *1–2 long green chilies, de-seeded and finely chopped*
- *1¾ litres (3½ pints) chicken stock*
- *125 g (4½ oz) red quinoa, rinsed and drained*
- *salt and pepper*
- *500 g (17½ oz) green shrimp (prawns), peeled and deveined*
- *240 ml (8 fl oz) milk*
- *3 tbsps chives, finely chopped*
- *lemon or lime juice (optional)*
- *cream (optional)*

Heat the oil in a large saucepan, and sauté onion until soft and slightly golden in color. Stir in the garlic and cook for 30 seconds.

Add the creamed and frozen corn, chilies and stock, stir, bring to the boil reduce the heat, cover and simmer on low-medium heat for 15 minutes.

Stir in the quinoa, season with salt to taste, bring back to the boil then reduce the heat, cover and simmer for another 15 minutes

Add the shrimp and milk, adjust the seasoning if need be and simmer covered for another 10 minutes.

Switch off the heat, stir in the chives and leave to rest covered for about 10 minutes before serving. The longer the soup is left to rest the more the quinoa will continue to absorb liquid and become thicker.

Serve with a squeeze of lemon or lime juice or stir through the cream, if you wish.

BACON, PEA AND LEEK SOUP

Serves 6–8

This soup is similar to the pea and ham soup that we all know and love except it's cooked in half the time and the addition of quinoa makes it hearty and filling. Wonderful for those cold, wintery days.

Ingredients

- *2 tbsp extra virgin olive oil*
- *250 g (9 oz) bacon, rind removed and cut into pieces*
- *1 large leek, washed and trimmed*
- *1 large onion, chopped*
- *1 kg (2 lb 4 oz) frozen peas*
- *2 litres (4½ fl oz) hot chicken or vegetable stock*
- *salt and freshly ground pepper*
- *140 g (5 oz) quinoa, rinsed and drained*

Heat oil in a large saucepan and cook bacon until browned and crispy but not dry or burnt. Remove from pan with a slotted spoon and set aside.

Chop the leek including the tender green part and add to the pan with the onion and sauté on low heat until lightly colored and soft.

Increase heat to high and add the peas (straight from the freezer) and the stock. Season to taste and bring to the boil. When boiling, reduce the heat to low, cover and simmer for about 15 minutes.

Purée the soup in a food processor or blender, return to the pot, increase heat to high and bring back to the boil.

Add the quinoa and the bacon, reduce heat and simmer for another 20 minutes until quinoa is cooked. Stir the pot occasionally.

I like to serve this soup with a drizzle of extra virgin olive oil and sometimes I might even cook up a little extra bacon for garnish.

SWEET POTATO SOUP

Serves 6–8

Ingredients

- *1 tbsp olive oil*
- *2 red onions, chopped*
- *1 tbsp ground cumin*
- *2 cloves garlic, chopped*
- *1–2 long red chilies, de-seeded, chopped*
- *zest of 1 lemon*
- *1.5 kg (3 lb 5 oz) sweet potato, peeled and chopped into chunks*
- *2 litres (4½ pints) hot chicken or vegetable stock*
- *salt and freshly cracked black pepper*
- *140 g (5 oz) quinoa, rinsed and drained*
- *480 ml (16 fl oz) boiling water, extra*

GARNISH

- *2 tbsp extra virgin olive oil*
- *1 large clove garlic, finely grated*
- *2 tsp ground cumin*
- *30 g (1 oz) fresh cilantro (coriander), finely chopped*
- *lemon juice*

Method

Heat oil in a large saucepan and sauté onion until soft. Stir in the cumin, garlic, chili and lemon zest and cook until fragrant.

Add the potato and stock and season to taste. Bring to the boil, reduce the heat, cover and simmer for 20–30 minutes until potato is tender.

Purée soup and bring back up to the boil, add the quinoa and extra water, reduce the heat, cover and simmer for 15–20 minutes until quinoa is cooked.

Stir in the garnish, check and adjust the seasoning. Serve with a good squeeze of lemon juice.

To make the garnish, heat the oil in a small frying pan and sauté the garlic until it just starts to change color. Add the cumin and cook until it starts to bubble. Stir in the cilantro and cook for a few seconds until the cilantro starts to wilt, then pour the garnish into the soup.

ZUCCHINI AND BACON SOUP

Serves 4–6

This is a thick and hearty soup, wonderful for those cold wintery days. If you think the soup may be too thick add a little hot water.

Ingredients

- *2 tbsps extra virgin olive oil*
- *300 g (10½ oz) bacon, rind removed and cut into pieces*
- *2 large onions, finely chopped*
- *2 tbsps tomato concentrate/paste*
- *1 kg (2 lb 4 oz) zucchini (courgette), coarsely grated*
- *2 cloves garlic, finely chopped*
- *2 litres (4½ pints) hot beef stock*
- *salt and freshly ground pepper*
- *140 g (5 oz) quinoa, rinsed and drained*
- *2–3 tbsps balsamic vinegar*
- *buffalo mozzarella, to serve*

Method

Heat oil in a large saucepan and sauté bacon on medium heat until it is lightly browned.

Add the onion and cook until soft. Stir in the tomato concentrate and cook for about 2 minutes.

Stir in the zucchini and garlic then pour in the stock and season with salt and pepper, keeping in mind that the bacon can be quite salty.

Bring to the boil, reduce the heat, cover and simmer for 5 minutes.

Add the quinoa, cover again and continue to simmer on low heat for another 30 minutes until the quinoa is cooked.

Stir the balsamic vinegar into the soup or, if preferred, everyone can add the vinegar individually into their own soup.

Serve garnished with some torn buffalo mozzarella cheese.

CREAMY CHICKEN AND LEEK SOUP

Serves 6

Thigh cutlets are the thigh with the back rib part of the bone removed and only the larger thigh bone left in. Because there is only one bone, I find using stock instead of water will give a far richer and tastier soup. I do like to use chicken thigh cutlets in this recipe as I feel thighs are better for soups and with just the larger bone in them the risk of finding smaller bones in the soup is less. But of course you can use whatever chicken pieces you prefer.

Ingredients

- *1 tbsp butter*
- *1–2 tbsps extra virgin olive oil*
- *2 large leeks, washed and sliced*
- *3 celery stalks, roughly chopped*
- *1 brown onion, chopped*
- *6 chicken thigh cutlets about 2 lb*
- *1.8 litres (4 pints) chicken stock or water*
- *pinch of ground cloves*
- *10–12 peppercorns*
- *140 g (5 oz) red quinoa, rinsed and drained*
- *salt and pepper*
- *120 ml (4 fl oz) cream*

Method

In a large saucepan, melt the butter and heat the oil until hot, then sauté the leeks, celery and onion until they soften and collapse and just start to take on some color.

Remove the skin from the chicken (optional) and add to the pot with the stock, cloves and peppercorns.

Bring to the boil, reduce the heat and simmer for about 30–40 minutes until chicken is cooked. Skim and remove any froth that rises during cooking.

Remove the chicken from the pot and set aside. Puree the soup and bring back to the boil.

When the soup is boiling, add the quinoa and season with salt. Reduce the heat, cover and simmer for about 20–30 minutes until the quinoa is cooked.

In the meantime, if you have left the skin on during cooking, remove the skin from the chicken and shred the meat into pieces.

Add the shredded chicken and cream to the soup and stir well. Taste and adjust the seasoning if necessary then continue to simmer on very, very low heat for 5 minutes until the chicken and cream have heated through.

Serve with a good grind of freshly cracked black pepper.

WILD MUSHROOMS, ZUCCHINI AND THYME SOUP

Serves 6–8

This is a very thick and hearty soup, wonderful on those cold wintry nights, especially if you love mushrooms. You can use any mushroom you like. Also, if you want to add a bit of crunch, sprinkle with some toasted quinoa.

Ingredients

- *2 tbsps extra virgin olive oil*
- *1 large brown onion, roughly chopped*
- *1 kg (2 lb 4 oz) selection of wild mushrooms, roughly chopped and the stalks removed if too woody*
- *750 g (1 lb 12 oz) zucchini (courgette), roughly chopped*
- *3 cloves garlic, roughly chopped*
- *2 tbsps thyme leaves*
- *salt and freshly ground black pepper*
- *zest of 1 lemon*
- *2 litres (4½ pints) vegetable or chicken stock*
- *240 ml (8 fl oz) boiling water*
- *125 g (4½ oz) quinoa, rinsed and drained*
- *lemon juice, for serving*
- *chives or thyme, chopped, for garnish*

Method

Heat the oil in a large saucepan and sauté onion until soft. Add the mushrooms, zucchini, garlic, thyme leaves, salt and pepper and cook until the vegetables have collapsed. The salt will help do this and draw out all the juices from the mushrooms.

Stir in the lemon zest and pour in the stock. Bring to the boil, reduce the heat and simmer for 30 minutes.

Puree the soup, bring back to the boil, pour in the water and stir in the quinoa. Reduce the heat, cover and simmer for 15–20 minutes until the quinoa is cooked.

Serve with a squeeze of lemon juice and a sprinkle of freshly chopped chives.

SWEET POTATO, CHILI, BASIL AND BALSAMIC VINEGAR BEAN SOUP

Serves 4–6

This is a thick and hearty soup. If you find it too thick, just add boiling water until you get the consistency you prefer.

Ingredients

- *2 tbsp olive oil*
- *1 large onion, chopped*
- *750 g (1 lb 8 oz) kumara (sweet potato), peeled and roughly cubed*
- *2–3 long red or green chilies, seeded and chopped*
- *1¼ litres (2½ pints) vegetable or chicken stock*
- *salt and freshly ground black pepper to taste*
- *80 g (3 oz) quinoa grain, rinsed and drained*
- *1 x 400 g (14 oz) can borlotti beans, drained and rinsed*
- *1 handful basil leaves, finely shredded*
- *2–3 tbsp balsamic vinegar*
- *extra chilies for garnish*

Heat the oil in a large saucepan and sauté the onion until golden. Add the sweet potato, chilies, stock, salt and pepper (check saltiness of stock before adding any salt). Bring to the boil, reduce the heat, cover, and simmer for about 20 minutes, until the sweet potato is tender.

Puree the soup in a blender and return to the saucepan. Add the quinoa and beans, bring back to the boil, reduce the heat and simmer, covered, for another 10–15 minutes.

Stir in the basil and balsamic vinegar and serve with a dish of finely sliced chilies.

Salads

PROSCIUTTO, BOCCONCINI AND FIG SALAD WITH HERBS

Serves 6

This is one of those salads that would be ideal for parties and special occasions. It is so easy to prepare yet looks beautiful when it's dressed and on a platter.

Ingredients

- *275 g (10 oz) quinoa, rinsed and drained*
- *700 ml (24 fl oz) water*
- *20 g (¾ oz) fresh chives, finely chopped*
- *20 g (¾ oz) mint, finely chopped*
- *150 g (5 oz) prosciutto, thinly sliced*
- *200 g (7 oz) bocconcini*
- *8 fresh ripe figs*
- *extra mint, for garnish*

DRESSING

- *1 tbsp Dijon mustard*
- *1 tbsp honey*
- *2 tbsps white or red wine vinegar*
- *75 ml (2½ fl oz) extra virgin olive oil*
- *salt and pepper*

Place the quinoa in a small saucepan with the water. Bring to the boil, reduce the heat, cover and simmer for 10 minutes until the quinoa is cooked and all the water is absorbed. Switch off the heat and leave to steam covered in the saucepan for about 10 minutes, then cool completely.

Place quinoa into a large bowl and using a fork lightly toss through the chives and the mint.

Whisk together the mustard, honey, vinegar, olive oil, salt and pepper. Pour ⅔ of the dressing over the quinoa and mix through. Reserve the remainder of the dressing to use just before serving.

When you are ready to serve, place the salad on a serving platter then loosely drape the prosciutto slices on top.

Tear the bocconcini in half and cut the figs into long quarters and arrange around and in the salad.

Sprinkle the top with some extra chopped mint and drizzle with the remaining dressing and an extra twist of freshly cracked pepper.

ARTICHOKE AND ARUGULA SALAD

Serves 4–8

Ingredients

- *185 g (6 oz) quinoa, rinsed and drained*
- *480 ml (16 fl oz) water*
- *2 x 280 g (10 oz) jars artichoke hearts, drained and halved*
- *2 x 400 g (14 oz) cans borlotti beans, rinsed and drained*
- *180 g (6 oz) pitted Kalamata olives, halved*
- *6 scallions (spring onions), sliced*
- *200 g (7 oz) arugula (rocket) leaves*

DRESSING

- *1 tbsp horseradish cream*
- *1 clove garlic, finely grated*
- *1–2 tbsp red wine vinegar*
- *3–4 tbsp extra virgin olive oil*
- *salt and freshly ground black pepper*

Method

Place quinoa in a small saucepan with the water, bring to the boil, then reduce the heat, cover and simmer for 10 minutes until all the water is absorbed. Remove from heat and cool.

Place quinoa in a bowl with the artichokes, beans, olives, shallots and arugula leaves and gently toss together to combine.

Whisk together the horseradish cream, garlic, red wine vinegar and olive oil. Season with salt and pepper.

Pour dressing over the salad and gently toss to combine.

ALMOND, CURRANT AND CARROT SALAD WITH A HONEYED YOGURT DRESSING

Serves 6-8

If you prefer, you can toss some of the dressing through the salad. Because the dressing is yogurt-based and therefore thicker than most dressings, I prefer to serve it on the side and let everyone help themselves.

Ingredients

- *275 g (10 oz) quinoa, rinsed and drained*
- *700 ml (24 fl oz) water*
- *80 g (3 oz) blanched almonds*
- *225 g (8 oz) dried currants*
- *3 medium-large carrots, coarsely grated*
- *1 red onion, finely chopped*
- *4 scallions (spring onions), sliced diagonally*
- *2 long red chilies, de-seeded and chopped*
- *30 g (1 oz) finely chopped flat-leaf parsley*
- *30 g (1 oz) finely chopped mint*

DRESSING

- *6 cardamom pods*
- *245 g (9 oz) natural Greek yogurt*
- *2 tsps honey*
- *60 ml (2 fl oz) extra virgin olive oil*
- *Juice of half a lemon*
- *2 tbsps red wine vinegar*
- *2 tsps curry powder*
- *½ tsp ground cumin*
- *salt and freshly ground black pepper*

Method

Place the quinoa in a medium saucepan with the water, bring to the boil, then reduce the heat, cover and simmer for 10 minutes until all the water is absorbed. Remove from heat, leave to stand covered for 10 minutes then cool completely.

Dry-roast almonds in a non-stick frying pan until golden; keep an eye on them as they can burn quickly once they start to color. Remove from pan and cool. Place quinoa into a large bowl with most of the almonds and most of the currants, then add the carrots, onion, scallions, chilies, parsley and mint.

For the dressing, break open the cardamom pods in a mortar and pestle then grind the seeds to a fine powder. Add to the remaining dressing ingredients, mix well and transfer to a small serving bowl. Place salad onto a serving platter and garnish with remaining almonds and currants. Serve with the dressing on the side.

BELL PEPPER, OLIVE AND GARLIC SALAD

Serves 4–6

This salad improves the longer it stands when all the flavors have had a chance to be absorbed.

Ingredients

- *185 g (6 oz) quinoa, rinsed and drained*
- *480 ml (16 fl oz) water*
- *1 large yellow bell pepper (capsicum)*
- *1 large red bell pepper (capsicum)*
- *1 large green bell pepper (capsicum)*
- *2 tbsps brown vinegar*
- *1 tsp brown sugar*
- *½–1 tsp dried chili flakes*
- *75 ml (2½ fl oz) extra virgin olive oil*
- *3–4 cloves garlic, sliced*
- *4 scallions (spring onions), finely sliced*
- *180 g (6 oz) black pitted Kalamata olives*
- *salt and freshly cracked black pepper*

Method

Place the quinoa in a small saucepan with the water. Bring to the boil, reduce the heat and simmer, covered, for 10 minutes until all the water is absorbed. Remove from the heat and leave, covered, for 10–15 minutes to steam. Cool completely.

Core and de-seed the bell peppers then slice into thin matchsticks and place into a deep bowl.

Mix together the vinegar, sugar and chili flakes and set aside.

Heat the oil in a small frying pan until hot and stir in the garlic. Cook for about 1 minute until it starts to take on some color.

Remove the pan from the heat and carefully add the vinegar mixture—it will more than likely splatter at this stage so be careful.

Return the pan to the heat for about 30 seconds then pour over the peppers and toss well. Cover with plastic film and leave to stand until cool.

Add the quinoa, scallions and olives to the bowl with the bell peppers and season with salt and pepper. Check and adjust seasoning and add more vinegar if you think it necessary. Toss the salad well and if possible refrigerate for about 30 minutes before serving.

PAPAYA WITH PROSCIUTTO, TOMATO, MINT AND CHIVES

Serves 4

This is a really nice dish for a special summer lunch although good anytime of the year. You can omit the prosciutto altogether for a refreshing vegetarian option.

Ingredients

- *125 g (4½ oz) white quinoa, rinsed and drained*
- *60 g (2½ oz) black quinoa, rinsed and drained*
- *480 ml (16 fl oz) water*
- *2 Lebanese cucumbers, cut into small pieces*
- *2 tomatoes, cut into small pieces*
- *3 tbsps mint, chopped*
- *3 tbsps chives, chopped*
- *6–8 slices prosciutto, cut into thin slices*
- *2 small to medium papaya, halved and seeded*
- *slices of limes, for decoration*

DRESSING

- *2 tbsps extra virgin olive oil*
- *juice and zest of ½ lime*
- *salt and freshly cracked black pepper*

Method

Place the quinoa into a small saucepan with the water. Bring to the boil, reduce the heat, cover and simmer for 12–15 minutes until all the water is absorbed. Remove from heat and leave to stand, covered, for 10–15 minutes then cool completely.

When quinoa has completely cooled, place in a bowl with the cucumbers, tomatoes, mint and chives.

To make the dressing, whisk together the oil, lime juice, zest, salt and pepper. Pour over the salad and gently toss, then add the prosciutto slices and gently mix through the salad.

Cut a very thin slice off the bottom of each papaya so that it will sit straight on the plate and remove all the seeds.

Fill each papaya half with the salad.

ROASTED PEPPER, BASIL AND PINE NUT SALAD

Serves 4–6

Use the whole roasted peppers in a jar and slice them yourself as opposed to using ones that are already sliced. I find the ready sliced ones don't drain as well and tend to retain too much of the liquid in the jar, making the salad go soggy.

Ingredients

- *185 g (6 oz) quinoa, rinsed and drained*
- *480 ml (16 fl oz) water*
- *125 g (4 oz) pine nuts*
- *250 g (9 oz) jar roasted bell peppers (capsicums), drained and sliced*
- *1 eschalot (French onion), chopped*
- *40 g (1½ oz) fresh basil leaves, chopped*
- *2–3 tbsps extra virgin olive oil*
- *1–2 tbsps raspberry red wine vinegar or red wine vinegar*
- *1 clove garlic, very finely grated*
- *salt and freshly cracked pepper*

Method

Place the quinoa in a small saucepan with the water. Bring to the boil, reduce the heat, cover and simmer for 10 minutes until the quinoa is cooked and all the water is absorbed. Leave to rest covered in the pan for 10 minutes before cooling completely.

Dry roast the pine nuts in a non-stick frying pan for a few minutes until they are a pale golden color. Keep an eye on them as they can burn very easily. Remove from the pan onto a plate and cool, otherwise they will continue to brown.

Place the quinoa and pine nuts into a large bowl. Add the peppers with the eschalots and basil. Whisk together the olive oil, vinegar and garlic then season with salt and pepper.

Pour over the salad and mix well until all the salad ingredients are coated with the dressing. Transfer onto a serving platter and serve.

Keep some of the pine nuts aside and use scattered over the salad as a garnish or dry roast some extra.

SMOKED TROUT AND FENNEL SALAD

Serves 4–6

This is a delicious salad for a luncheon if you are having guests and you want something a little more special to serve. You can use smoked salmon instead of the trout and for a quick meal at home you can prepare this salad using a good-quality tinned red salmon.

Ingredients

- *185 g (6 oz) quinoa, rinsed and drained*
- *480 ml (16 fl oz) water*
- *2 small baby fennel bulbs*
- *2 Lebanese cucumbers*
- *250 g (9 oz) small cherry or grape tomatoes, left whole*
- *4–6 scallions (spring onions), sliced*
- *20 g (¾ oz) finely chopped dill*
- *400 g (14 oz) smoked trout, flaked*
- *extra dill, chopped, for serving*

DRESSING

- *90 g (3 oz) sundried tomatoes*
- *1 tsp horseradish (from a jar)*
- *1 small clove garlic, very finely grated*
- *1–2 tbsps white wine vinegar*
- *4 tbsps extra virgin olive oil*
- *salt and white pepper to taste*

Place the quinoa in a small saucepan with the water. Bring to the boil, reduce the heat, cover and simmer for 10 minutes until all the water is absorbed. Remove from the heat and leave covered to steam for about 10 minutes.

Trim the fennel bulbs by removing any damaged outer leaves. Then cut in half and slice very finely (baby fennel usually need very little, if any, trimming as they are very young and tender).

Slice the cucumbers in quarters lengthways, then dice and place into a bowl with the fennel, tomatoes, scallions and dill. Add the cooled quinoa and gently toss.

Make the dressing by placing the sundried tomatoes, horseradish, garlic, vinegar and oil into a blender or food processor and process until smooth, then season with salt and pepper.

Pour most of the dressing over the salad and toss with a fork to combine then transfer onto a serving platter. Drape slices of the trout decoratively over and in the salad, drizzle with the remaining dressing and extra chopped dill before serving.

TOMATO AND MOZZARELLA PESTO SALAD

Serves 4–6

Ingredients

- *275 g (10 oz) quinoa, rinsed and drained*
- *700 ml (24 fl oz) water*
- *250 g (9 oz) grape or cherry tomatoes*
- *220 g (8 oz) baby bocconcini cheese*
- *lemon juice*
- *olive oil, extra*
- *parmesan, shaved*
- *basil leaves, for garnish*

PESTO SAUCE

- *1 large bunch basil leaves*
- *2 cloves garlic, chopped*
- *90 g (3 oz) pine nuts*
- *140 g (5 oz) parmesan, freshly grated*
- *120 ml (4 fl oz) extra virgin olive oil*
- *salt and pepper*

Place quinoa in a small saucepan with the water, bring to the boil, then reduce the heat, cover and simmer for 10 minutes until all the water is absorbed. Remove from the heat and cool completely.

To make the pesto, place basil, garlic, pine nuts and cheese into a food processor or blender. With the motor on pulse mode, slowly pulse the ingredients and pour in enough oil until you get a creamy and soft consistency that still has a little texture to it.

Season to taste and add more cheese or oil if needed according to your preference. If feeling particularly energetic you can use a mortar and pestle to make the sauce.

Place the quinoa into a bowl and mix in the pesto sauce really well so as to completely coat the quinoa.

Leave the tomatoes whole or cut in half and roughly tear the cheese open without cutting through completely. Toss the tomatoes and mozzarella through the quinoa.

Squeeze some lemon juice on top and serve garnished with shavings of parmesan, basil leaves and a light drizzle of extra virgin olive oil.

CRANBERRY AND SWEET POTATO SALAD

Serves 4–6

I love the look of this salad and it's ideal for a gathering as it has a colorful party look about it.

Ingredients

- *1 kg (2 lb 4 oz) orange sweet potato,*
- *extra virgin olive oil*
- *salt and pepper*
- *185 g (6 oz) quinoa, rinsed and drained*
- *480 ml (16 fl oz) water*
- *150 g (5 oz) dried cranberries*
- *juice of 1 orange, strained*
- *2 Lebanese cucumbers, diced*
- *3 tbsps mint, chopped*

DRESSING

- *1 tbsp honey*
- *1 tsp Dijon mustard*
- *2 tbsps extra virgin olive oil*
- *salt and freshly ground black pepper*

Method

Preheat oven to 200°C (400°F) and line a baking tray with baking parchment/paper.

Peel the sweet potato and dice, place onto the baking tray and drizzle with a little olive oil and season with salt and pepper. Gently toss the sweet potato so as to cover with the oil and the seasoning. Bake for about 20 minutes until tender but still with a little bite to it. You don't want them too soft or they will turn to mush.

Place quinoa into a small saucepan with the water. Bring to the boil, reduce the heat and simmer, covered for 10 minutes or until the water is absorbed. Remove from the heat and leave covered to steam for about 10–15 minutes then cool completely.

In the meantime, soak the cranberries in the orange juice for 10 minutes, strain and reserve the juice.

When the quinoa has cooled, place into a large bowl with the sweet potato, cranberries, cucumbers and mint.

Whisk together the reserved orange juice, honey, mustard, olive oil, salt and pepper.

Pour the dressing over the salad and gently toss to thoroughly mix everything together.

MEXICAN CORN AND RED KIDNEY BEAN SALAD

Serves 4–6

You can use fresh or frozen corn kernels. If using frozen, make sure they are fully thawed and dry before placing in the frying pan to toast.

Ingredients

- *90 g (3½ oz) quinoa grain, rinsed and drained*
- *240 ml (8 fl oz) water*
- *300 g (10½ oz) fresh corn kernels*
- *½ large red pepper (capsicum), diced*
- *½ large green pepper (capsicum), diced*
- *1 small red onion, halved and thinly sliced*
- *1 x 400 g (14 oz) can red kidney beans, rinsed and drained*
- *80g (3 oz) chopped cilantro (coriander)*

MEXICAN DRESSING

- *¼ tsp dried ground oregano*
- *¼ tsp ground cumin*
- *¼ tsp paprika*
- *finely chopped fresh chili to taste*
- *juice of 1 lime*
- *4 tbsp extra virgin olive oil*
- *salt and freshly ground black pepper to taste*

Method

Place the quinoa in a small saucepan with the water, bring to the boil, then reduce the heat, cover and simmer for 10 minutes until all the water is absorbed. Remove from the heat and cool completely.

Dry-toast the corn in a non-stick frying pan until it turns golden, then remove from the heat and cool.

Place the quinoa, corn, red and green peppers, onion, red kidney beans and cilantro in a bowl and mix well.

Whisk all the dressing ingredients together and pour over salad. Toss well and serve.

POMEGRANATE, APRICOT, PISTACHIO AND PINE NUT SALAD

Serves 6

This is one of my favorite salads and so colorful. The pomegranate gives it a real jewelled effect, ideal to be used as a Christmas salad.

Ingredients

- *140 g (5 oz) quinoa, rinsed and drained*
- *350 ml (12 fl oz) water*
- *90 g (3 oz) pine nuts, lightly toasted*
- *1 large pomegranate*
- *150 g (5 oz) dried apricots, chopped*
- *150 g (5 oz) shelled unsalted pistachios*
- *1 small red onion, finely chopped*
- *20 g (¾ oz) chopped mint*
- *20 g (¾ oz) chopped flat-leaf parsley*
- *juice of 1 lemon*
- *2 tbsp extra virgin olive oil*
- *salt and freshly cracked black pepper*

Method

Place the quinoa in a small saucepan with the water, bring to the boil, reduce the heat, cover and simmer for 10 minutes until all the water is absorbed. Remove from the heat and leave to stand covered for at least 10 minutes, then cool completely.

In the meantime, lightly dry roast the pine nuts in a non-stick frying pan until they just start to change color. Remove from the pan onto another dish so as to cool and stop the cooking process.

Cut the pomegranate in half and using the back of a wooden spoon, bash each half over and into a large bowl to release the fruit and collect the juice.

Add the cooled quinoa into the bowl with the pine nuts, apricots, pistachio nuts and onion.

Mix in the herbs, lemon juice and oil, then season with salt and pepper to taste. Toss well and refrigerate for 30 minutes before serving. The pistachios can be added just before serving as they can go a little soft if sitting in the dressing for too long.

ROASTED SWEET POTATO, SPINACH AND MUSHROOM SALAD

Serves 4–8

This is a big and hearty salad and is a meal on its own. The number of serves depends on whether you are serving it on its own or as a side dish.

Ingredients

- *1 kg (2 lb 4 oz) sweet potato*
- *1–2 tbsp extra virgin olive oil*
- *salt and pepper*
- *140 g (5 oz) red quinoa, rinsed and drained*
- *350 ml (12 fl oz) water*
- *200 g (7 oz) baby spinach leaves*
- *250 g (9 oz) mushrooms, sliced*
- *1 red onion, halved and thinly sliced*

DRESSING

- *2 tbsp Dijon mustard*
- *juice of 1–2 lemons*
- *120 ml (4 fl oz) extra virgin olive oil*
- *salt and freshly ground black pepper*

Preheat oven to 180°C (350°F) and line a baking tray with non-stick baking paper.

Peel and cube sweet potato, drizzle with olive oil and season with salt and pepper. Toss well and place on the baking tray in a single layer.

Roast in the oven for 20–30 minutes until potato is tender and browned.

In the meantime, place quinoa in a small saucepan with the water, bring to the boil, then reduce the heat, cover and simmer for 10–12 minutes until all the water is absorbed. Remove from heat and cool.

Place sweet potato, quinoa, spinach, mushroom and onion in a bowl and gently toss together until combined.

Mix together all dressing ingredients, pour over salad and gently toss. Leave to stand for about ½ hour before serving.

COLESLAW

Serves 8–10

This makes a large salad and is great for a crowd. The quinoa adds an extra crunch and texture, especially as I have used the black quinoa, which tends to remain crunchier than the white one.

Ingredients

- *185 g (6 oz) black quinoa, rinsed and drained*
- *480 ml (16 fl oz) water*
- *¼ small white cabbage, trimmed and finely shredded*
- *¼ small red cabbage, trimmed and finely shredded*
- *2 carrots, coarsely grated*
- *1 red onion, halved and finely sliced*
- *2 stalks celery, finely sliced*
- *salt and freshly cracked pepper*
- *110 g (4 oz) mayonnaise*
- *2 tbsp red wine vinegar*
- *2 tbsp extra virgin olive oil*

Method

Place quinoa in a small saucepan with the water, bring to the boil, then reduce the heat, cover and simmer for 10–14 minutes until all the water is absorbed and the quinoa is tender. Remove from heat and cool completely.

Combine the quinoa, cabbages, carrots, onion and celery in a large bowl and mix really well—your hands are probably the best mixing tool for this salad.

Stir through the mayonnaise, vinegar and olive oil, season with salt and pepper and toss until well coated.

Cover and chill for several hours before serving.

SHRIMP AND AVOCADO SALAD

Serves 4–6

This is a lovely summer salad that can also be served as an entrée.

Ingredients

- *140 g (5 oz) red quinoa grain, rinsed and drained*
- *350 ml (12 fl oz) water*
- *750 g (1 lb 10 oz) cooked shrimp (prawns)*
- *2 stalks celery, finely sliced*
- *20 g (¾ oz) chopped flatleaf parsley*
- *2 long red chilies, sliced*
- *2 large avocados, peeled and cut into chunks*
- *60 ml (2 fl oz) extra virgin olive oil*
- *2 tbsp balsamic vinegar*
- *salt to taste*

Place the quinoa in a small saucepan with the water, bring to the boil, then reduce the heat, cover and simmer for 10 minutes until all the water is absorbed. Remove from the heat and cool completely.

Peel and devein shrimp, leaving the tails intact. Place in a large bowl with the quinoa, celery, parsley, chilies and avocados and gently toss to combine.

Mix the olive oil, vinegar and salt together, pour over the salad and toss well. Allow the flavors to combine for about 30 minutes before serving. Adjust dressing to suit your taste if necessary.

BRUSCHETTA SALAD

Serves 4–6

The beautiful vibrant colors in this salad make it ideal to serve for lunch. Here I've paired it with some delicious Herb-crusted Veal Schnitzel (see recipe page 216).

Ingredients

- *140 g (5 oz) black quinoa grain, rinsed and drained*
- *90 g (3½ oz) white quinoa grain, rinsed and drained*
- *590 ml (20 fl oz) water*
- *250 g (9 oz) small grape or cherry tomatoes, halved*
- *1 small red onion, finely chopped*
- *40 g (1½ oz) fresh basil leaves*
- *2 tbsps balsamic vinegar*
- *1 tbsp red wine vinegar*
- *1 small clove garlic, very finely grated*
- *4–5 tbsps extra virgin olive oil*
- *salt and freshly ground black pepper*

Method

Place the quinoa in a small-medium saucepan with the water. Bring to the boil, reduce the heat, cover and simmer for 12–15 minutes until the quinoa is cooked and all the water is absorbed.

Switch off the heat and stand covered until it cools completely. If the water dries out during the cooking time add a little more. Keep in mind that the white quinoa will cook in less time than the black and will have a softer texture.

Place the cooled quinoa into a bowl with the tomatoes and onion.

Finely chop the basil and stir into the salad. In a separate bowl whisk together the balsamic and red wine vinegar, garlic and olive oil then season well with salt and pepper. Pour over the salad and toss really well.

If possible prepare the salad at least 2 hours before serving as the flavors will blend in and develop more.

BEETROOT GARDEN SALAD

Serves 6–10

This salad is an all-time favorite and looks stunning on a white platter. It's great for barbeques. Home-cooked beetroot is best to use and well worth the effort. If you must use the tinned variety, whole beetroot is better than the slices.

Ingredients

- *140 g (5 oz) quinoa grain, rinsed and drained*
- *350 ml (12 fl oz) water*
- *500 g (1 lb 2 oz) cooked beetroot, diced*
- *2 celery stalks, finely sliced*
- *½ pepper (capsicum), diced*
- *1 medium carrot, finely diced*
- *1 large red onion, finely chopped*
- *4 scallions (spring onions), finely sliced*
- *2–3 radishes, finely sliced*
- *1 x 400 g (14 oz) can cannellini beans, rinsed and drained*
- *40 g (1½ oz) chopped flatleaf parsley*

DRESSING

- *1 clove garlic*
- *salt and ground black pepper to taste*
- *2 tbsp red wine vinegar*
- *5 tbsp extra virgin olive oil*

Place the quinoa in a small saucepan with the water, bring to the boil, then reduce the heat, cover and simmer for 10 minutes until all the water is absorbed. Remove from the heat and cool completely. Place the cooled quinoa in a large bowl with all other salad ingredients.

To make dressing: place the garlic, seasoning, vinegar and olive oil in a mortar and pestle and pound until blended or very finely grate the garlic and mix with the other ingredients. Adjust quantities to taste. Pour over the salad and toss gently to combine.

SALAMI, ROASTED PEPPERS, SUNDRIED TOMATO AND OLIVE SALAD

Serves 4–6

For a vegetarian option, leave out the salami. I tend to add anchovies as I absolutely love them and they go so well in this salad.

Ingredients

- *140 g (5 oz) quinoa grain, rinsed and drained*
- *350 ml (12 fl oz) water*
- *250 g (8 oz) mushrooms, sliced*
- *3 scallions (spring onions), sliced*
- *125 g (4 oz) sundried tomatoes, sliced*
- *125 g (4 oz) roasted pepper (capsicum), sliced*
- *2 tbsp capers, drained*
- *24 kalamata olives, pitted*
- *125 g (4 oz) salami, cut into pieces*
- *1 clove garlic, very finely grated*
- *20 g (¾ oz) chopped basil*
- *20 g (¾ oz) chopped flatleaf parsley*
- *2 tbsp balsamic vinegar*
- *4–5 tbsp extra virgin olive oil*
- *salt and freshly ground black pepper*

Method

Place the quinoa in a small saucepan with the water, bring to the boil, then reduce the heat, cover and simmer for 10 minutes until all the water is absorbed. Remove from heat and cool completely.

Place the cooled quinoa in a large bowl with all other ingredients.Toss well and let all the flavors combine for about 30 minutes before serving.

CHICKEN SALAD

Serves 4 as a main meal

Ingredients

- *2 chicken breast fillets*
- *185 g (6 oz) quinoa grain, rinsed and drained*
- *480 ml (16 fl oz) chicken stock or water*
- *3 tbsp chopped parsley*
- *2 tbsp chopped chives*
- *1 tsp finely chopped rosemary*
- *20 black kalamata olives, pitted and halved*
- *1 punnet cherry tomatoes cut in half*
- *2 tbsp balsamic vinegar*
- *4 tbsp extra virgin olive oil*
- *1 generous tbsp horseradish cream*
- *salt and freshly ground black pepper*

Preheat the oven to 170°C (325°F).

Rub the chicken breasts with a little olive oil and season with salt and pepper. Place on a baking tray and roast in the oven for about 15 minutes, until cooked. Remove from the oven, cover with foil and allow to rest.

Place the quinoa in a small saucepan with the stock or water, bring to the boil, then reduce the heat, cover and simmer for 10 minutes until all the water is absorbed. Remove from the heat and cool completely.

When the quinoa has cooled, place it in a salad bowl. Using two forks, shred the chicken into bite-sized pieces and add to the bowl with the parsley, chives, rosemary and olives. Gently squeeze out the seeds from the cherry tomatoes and add the tomato flesh to the bowl .

Whisk the vinegar, olive oil, horseradish cream, salt and pepper together, pour over into the salad, toss gently and serve.

MEDITERRANEAN SUMMER SALAD

Serves 4–6

This is a lovely salad and great as an accompaniment with meat or fish. You can roast your own peppers or buy them ready roasted or chargrilled. The anchovies add an extra zing to the dressing but you can leave them out. This has all the true flavors of the Mediterranean.

Ingredients

- *140 g (5 oz) quinoa grain, rinsed and drained*
- *350 ml (12 fl oz) water*
- *90 g (3½ oz) pitted black kalamata olives*
- *2 tbsp capers, drained*
- *125 g (4 oz) sun-dried tomatoes, sliced*
- *150 g (5 oz) roasted pepper (capsicum), cut into chunks*
- *280 g (9 oz) artichoke hearts, quartered*
- *1 x 400 g (14 oz) can borlotti beans, rinsed and drained*
- *1 green chili, seeded and chopped*
- *1 small red onion, finely chopped*
- *2 tbsp chopped chives*
- *20 g (¾ oz) chopped dill*

DRESSING

- *2 anchovy fillets (optional)*
- *4 tbsp extra virgin olive oil*
- *1½–2 tbsp red wine vinegar*
- *2 cloves garlic*
- *salt and freshly ground black*
- *pepper to taste*

Method

Place the quinoa in a small saucepan with the water, bring to the boil, then reduce the heat, cover and simmer for 10 minutes until all the water is absorbed. Remove from the heat and cool completely.

Halve the olives lengthways and place in a large bowl with quinoa, capers, sun-dried tomatoes, peppers, artichokes, beans, chili, onion and herbs. Mix thoroughly.

For the dressing, place the anchovies, olive oil, vinegar, garlic and seasoning in a blender or mortar and pestle and whiz or grind together until blended.

Pour the dressing over the salad, check the seasoning (you will need to add salt if not using the anchovies). Chill for about 30 minutes before serving.

CUCUMBER, FRESH COCONUT, LIME AND CHILI SALAD

Serves 4–6

Ingredients

- *140 g (5 oz) red quinoa, rinsed and drained*
- *350 ml (12 fl oz) water*
- *4 Lebanese cucumbers, halved and sliced diagonally*
- *75 g (3 oz) freshly grated coconut*
- *1 eschalot (French shallot), finely chopped*
- *2 scallions (spring onions), sliced diagonally*
- *2 long red chilies, de-seeded and chopped*

DRESSING

- *juice of 2–3 limes*
- *3 tsps fish sauce*
- *1 tsp sugar*
- *1 tbsp extra virgin olive oil*

Method

Place the quinoa in a small saucepan with the water, bring to the boil, cover, reduce the heat and simmer for 10–13 minutes until the quinoa is cooked and all the water is absorbed. Cool completely.

Place the cucumbers (you can remove the seeds from the cucumber if you prefer, I like to leave them in), coconut, eschalots, scallions and chilies into a large bowl with the quinoa. If you don't mind the extra heat you can leave the seeds in the chilies.

Prepare the dressing by mixing together the lime juice, fish sauce, sugar and oil. Pour the dressing over the salad and toss really well.

Stand at room temperature for about 30 minutes before serving so that all the flavors combine.

TUNA SALAD

Serves 4–6

This is my son's favorite salad and he takes it to work two to three times every week. It is filling and satisfying. I often have it in the fridge and everyone uses it as a meal on the run or just as a quick snack.

Ingredients

- *185 g (6 oz) quinoa, rinsed and drained*
- *480 ml (16 fl oz) water*
- *1 red bell pepper (capsicum), cut into chunks*
- *1 green bell pepper (capsicum), cut into chunks*
- *2 Lebanese cucumbers, diced*
- *6 scallions (spring onions), sliced*
- *3 tbsps parsley, finely chopped*
- *2–3 tablespons capers, drained*
- *15–20 pitted Kalamata olives, halved*
- *2 x 400 g (14 oz) cans cannellini beans, rinsed and drained*
- *1 x 400 g (14 oz) can tuna chunks in spring water or oil, drained*

DRESSING

- *1½ tbsp red wine vinegar*
- *3 tablespons extra virgin olive oil*
- *Salt and freshly ground black pepper*

Method

Place the quinoa in a small saucepan with the water, bring to the boil, then reduce the heat, cover and simmer for 10 minutes until all the water is absorbed. Remove from heat and cool completely.

Combine the quinoa with the bell peppers, cucumbers, scallions, parsley, capers, olives and beans in a bowl and toss well.

Drain the tuna and add to the salad: you can use either tuna in spring water or oil, totally up to you.

Whisk together the vinegar, oil, salt and pepper. Pour over salad and toss through.

AVOCADO SALAD WITH TOASTED QUINOA AND A BALSAMIC VINAIGRETTE DRESSING

Serves 4

Toasted quinoa goes particularly well with a quick tossed salad. It adds body, texture and crunch to an otherwise basic dish. The dressing can be stored in the refrigerator in a jar with a lid. Vary the ingredients below to suit your tastes and seasonal produce.

Ingredients

- *2 avocadoes, peeled and diced*
- *2 small Lebanese cucumbers, sliced*
- *1 red onion, thinly sliced*
- *selection of mesclun/mixed gourmet salad leaves*
- *250 g (9 oz) grape or cherry tomatoes*
- *185 g (6 oz) toasted quinoa (see page 27)*
- *extra toasted quinoa, for garnish*

DRESSING

- *60 ml (2 fl oz) good balsamic vinegar*
- *2 tsps Dijon mustard*
- *2 tbsps honey*
- *1 clove garlic, very finely grated*
- *salt*
- *175 ml (6 fl oz) extra virgin olive oil*
- *freshly cracked black pepper*

Method

Prepare the dressing first by whisking the vinegar, mustard, honey, garlic, and salt together until the salt has dissolved.

Slowly add the olive oil, whisking constantly until you have a runny but thick dressing. Stir in the pepper, then taste and adjust the seasoning.

Place all of your salad ingredients in a bowl with a few tbsps of the dressing and toss well.

Place on to a serving platter and garnish with extra toasted quinoa and serve immediately. Serve the remaining salad dressing in a jug for people to help themselves.

Vegetarian

SPINACH WITH LENTILS AND PINE NUTS

Serves 6

This is a lovely vegetarian dish that re-heats beautifully. I prefer to add the chilies as a garnish instead of stirring the chilies into the dish. That way any children who don't like chili can still eat the dish and everyone else gets as much or as little chili as they like.

Ingredients

- *125 g (4 oz) pine nuts*
- *1 tbsp extra virgin olive oil*
- *6 scallions (spring onions), finely chopped*
- *2–3 cloves garlic, finely chopped*
- *2 x 400 g (14 oz) cans brown lentils, rinsed and drained*
- *370 g (12½ oz) quinoa, rinsed and drained*
- *950 ml (32 fl oz) hot vegetable stock*
- *Salt and freshly ground black pepper*
- *250 g (9 oz) fresh baby spinach leaves*
- *lemon juice, for serving*
- *natural Greek yogurt, for serving*
- *red chilies, sliced for garnish (optional)*

Method

Dry-roast the pine nuts in a small non-stick frying pan until lightly browned. Remove from the pan and set aside. Don't be tempted to leave them in the pan, as they will continue to brown in the residual heat.

Heat oil in a large saucepan and sauté scallions until soft, stir in the garlic and cook for 1–2 minutes.

Add the lentils and quinoa, give the pot a good stir, then pour in the hot stock and season with a little salt and pepper, keeping in mind that stock is normally salty.

Bring to the boil, reduce heat, cover and simmer for 20 minutes until almost all the liquid has been absorbed.

Stir in the spinach, cover and continue simmering on low heat for another 5 minutes. Using a fork, stir in the pine nuts, cover then remove off the heat and leave for about 10 minutes before serving with a good squeeze of lemon juice and a dollop of yogurt.

Garnish with a few slices of red chilies.

SPINACH AND CHEESE SOUFFLÉ

Serves 4

The soufflé can be prepared in advance up to the stage where the egg whites are to be whisked and folded in. However, you will have to reheat the spinach mixture beforehand, otherwise the soufflé will not rise. Cover the spinach mixture with plastic wrap to stop skin from forming.

Ingredients

- ▶ *grated parmesan cheese*
- ▶ *250 g (8 oz) frozen spinach leaves, thawed*
- ▶ *1 tsp butter, plus 2½ tbsp*
- ▶ *3 tbsp quinoa flour*
- ▶ *240 ml (8 fl oz) hot milk*
- ▶ *a pinch of nutmeg*
- ▶ *4 extra-large egg yolks*
- ▶ *90 g (3 oz) grated sharp or vintage cheddar cheese*
- ▶ *30 g (1 oz) grated parmesan cheese*
- ▶ *salt and pepper*
- ▶ *5 extra-large egg whites*
- ▶ *a pinch salt*
- ▶ *a pinch cream of tartar*

Preheat the oven to 190°C (375°F). Butter 4 x 240 ml (8 fl oz) capacity ramekins, then sprinkle liberally with grated parmesan cheese.

Place the spinach in a fine sieve and press with the back of a spoon to remove all moisture. Melt 1 tsp of butter in a small frying pan, add the spinach and cook on low heat for 2–3 minutes, stirring occasionally, to allow any excess moisture to evaporate. Remove from the heat.

Melt 2½ tbsp butter in a saucepan, stir in the flour to form a roux and cook for about 30 seconds, stirring constantly. Gradually stir in the milk and nutmeg and continue cooking, stirring constantly, until thickened. Remove from the heat and add the egg yolks one at a time, mixing well, then stir in the cheeses. Keep stirring until the cheese has melted then season. Using a spatula, gently fold in the spinach.

Whisk the egg whites with the salt and cream of tartar until stiff and soft peaks form. Fold two large spoonfuls of egg whites into the spinach mixture to loosen it, then fold in the remaining egg whites using a metal spoon. Spoon the mixture into the ramekins. Separate the soufflé mixture from the rim of the dishes by running your finger along the edge—this will help it rise more evenly.

Place the ramekins on the middle shelf of the heated oven and bake for 25 minutes until well risen and just set. Serve immediately.

Vegetarian

CARDAMOM, CHILI AND MUSTARD SEED PILAF

Serves 4-6

This dish is filling as a vegetarian meal on its own or as a side dish with meat, fish or chicken.

Ingredients

- *6–8 cardamom pods or about ½–1 tsp powdered, according to taste*
- *1 tbsp olive oil*
- *1 tbsp ghee*
- *2 tsps mustard seeds*
- *1 large onion, halved, thinly sliced*
- *1 tbsp grated fresh ginger*
- *3 cloves garlic, finely chopped*
- *1 tsp ground cumin*
- *½ tsp cinnamon*
- *½ tsp saffron strands*
- *950 ml (32 fl oz) hot water*
- *370 g (12½ oz) quinoa, rinsed and drained*
- *salt and freshly ground black pepper*
- *2 long red chilies, de-seeded and chopped*
- *30 g (1 oz) chopped fresh cilantro (coriander) leaves*
- *juice 1–2 limes*
- *lime wedges, for serving*

Method

Break open the cardamom pods and, using a mortar and pestle, grind the seeds to a fine powder and set aside.

Heat the oil and melt the ghee in a large deep-frying pan, add the mustard seeds and cook until they start to pop then add the onion and cook until soft.

Stir in the ginger and garlic and cook for about 30 seconds. Add the ground cardamom, cumin and cinnamon.

Mix the saffron strands with the hot water and let them steep for a few seconds then add to the pan with the quinoa. Stir well and season with salt and pepper. Bring to the boil, cover and simmer on low heat for about 15–20 minutes until all the water is absorbed.

Turn off the heat and leave to stand for about 5 minutes then, using a fork, stir through the chilies, cilantro leaves and lime juice.

Serve with lime wedges.

MIDDLE EASTERN BEAN PATTIES WITH YOGURT AND MINT SAUCE

Makes 8–10 patties

Ingredients

- *90 g (3½ oz) quinoa grain, rinsed and drained*
- *240 ml (8 fl oz) water*
- *2 x 400 g (14 oz) cans red kidney beans*
- *3 cloves garlic, grated*
- *4 scallions (spring onions), finely sliced*
- *1 tsp ground cumin*
- *½–1 tsp chili powder*
- *3 tbsp chopped cilantro (coriander)*
- *1 egg*
- *salt to taste*
- *2 tbsp olive oil*
- *yogurt Salsa*
- *125 g (4½ oz) Greek yogurt*
- *1 tbsp finely chopped mint*
- *1 tsp extra virgin olive oil*
- *salt and pepper to taste*

Place the quinoa in a small saucepan with the water. Bring to the boil, then reduce the heat, cover and simmer for 10 minutes until all the water is absorbed. Remove from the heat and cool.

Rinse and drain the red kidney beans and coarsely mash with fork or potato masher and place in a bowl. Add the cooked quinoa, garlic, shallots, cumin, chili, cilantro and egg, season with salt and mix until all the ingredients are well combined. Divide the mixture into 8 or 10 and shape into round patties.

Heat the olive oil in a non-stick frying pan over medium heat. Add the patties and cook until golden on both sides, about 3–4 minutes each side.

To make the sauce, mix together the yogurt, mint and extra virgin olive oil, and season with salt and pepper if you wish.

Serve the bean patties with the yogurt mint sauce and a garden salad.

Vegetarian

SAVORY ZUCCHINI, TOMATOES AND BLACK BEANS WITH BASIL

Serves 4-6

Ingredients

- *3 tbsps extra virgin olive oil*
- *250 g (9 oz) small grape or cherry tomatoes*
- *1 large red onion, chopped*
- *3 medium zucchini (courgette), sliced*
- *3 cloves garlic, chopped*
- *275 g (10 oz) quinoa, rinsed and drained*
- *salt and pepper*
- *590 ml (20 fl oz) hot vegetable stock or water*
- *200 g (7 oz) fresh baby spinach leaves*
- *2 x 400 g (14 oz) can black beans, drained*
- *small handful of fresh basil leaves, thinly sliced*
- *balsamic vinegar (optional)*

Heat the oil in a large frying pan, add the tomatoes and toss gently in the oil to slightly cook and blister the skin about 3–4 minutes. Remove from the pan and set aside.

Add the onion and zucchini to the pan and sauté until onions are soft and golden and zucchini lightly browned.

Stir in garlic and quinoa, and season with salt and pepper. Pour in the stock, bring to the boil, reduce the heat, cover and simmer for 15 minutes until all the liquid is absorbed and the quinoa is cooked.

Stir in the spinach and, once it has wilted, return the tomatoes to the pan with the beans and basil and gently mix through.

Simmer, covered, for another 3–5 minutes until the beans and tomatoes are heated through then take off the heat and leave for about 5 minutes before serving.

For an added tang, I like to drizzle some balsamic vinegar over the top before serving.

LEMON, GINGER, TURMERIC AND CURRY LEAF PILAF

Serves 4–6

Ingredients

- *370 g (12½ oz) quinoa, rinsed and drained*
- *950 ml (32 fl oz) water*
- *2 tbsp olive oil*
- *1 tbsp black mustard seeds*
- *1–2 tbsp ginger, grated*
- *3 cloves garlic, grated*
- *½–1 tsp dried chili flakes*
- *1 tsp ground turmeric*
- *salt*
- *handful of fresh curry leaves*
- *juice of 1–2 lemons*
- *fresh red chilies, sliced, for garnish (optional)*

Place quinoa into a medium-sized saucepan with the water, bring to the boil, then reduce the heat, cover and simmer for 10 minutes until all the water is absorbed. Remove from heat.

Heat oil in a large frying pan, add the mustard seeds and cook on medium-high heat until they start to pop. Add the ginger, garlic and chili flakes and cook until fragrant, about 1–2 minutes, then stir in the turmeric and season with salt.

Lightly crush the curry leaves to release their natural oil and add to the pan, cook 1–2 minutes until they start to release their fragrance and collapse.

Stir in the quinoa and lemon juice and mix really well until everything is thoroughly combined and heated through.

Garnish with the fresh chilies if used and serve the pilaf on its own or as a side dish.

WILD MUSHROOMS WITH WINE AND GARLIC

Serves 4

You can use a combination of a variety of mushrooms or you can use just one type—it really doesn't matter. I usually choose a combination of ordinary field mushrooms, Swiss brown, fresh shiitake, Portobello, oyster or enoki. Any type of mushroom works really well.

Ingredients

- *2 tbsp extra virgin olive oil*
- *1 kg (2 lb 4 oz) selection of wild mushrooms*
- *1 large brown onion, finely chopped*
- *4 scallions (spring onions), sliced*
- *3 cloves garlic, finely chopped*
- *120 ml (4 fl oz) white wine*
- *275 g (10 oz) quinoa grain, rinsed and drained*
- *590 ml (20 fl oz) hot water*
- *salt and freshly cracked black pepper*
- *20 g (¾ oz) flat-leaf parsley, finely chopped*
- *parmesan, shaved*

Method

Heat oil in a large, deep-sided frying pan. Slice the larger mushrooms and leave any tiny ones whole then toss in the oil and cook until they have collapsed and are soft, about 3–5 minutes.

Remove the mushrooms from the pan with a slotted spoon and set aside.

Add onion and scallions to the pan and sauté until golden; add a little more oil to the pan if necessary.

Stir in the garlic and cook for a few seconds then pour in the wine and deglaze the pan. Cook for about 1–2 minutes until the alcohol evaporates. Add the quinoa, one-third of the mushrooms and the water.

Season with salt and pepper then bring to the boil, reduce the heat, cover and simmer for about 12–15 minutes until all the water is absorbed and the quinoa is cooked.

Toss in the parsley and remaining mushrooms and serve with shavings of parmesan.

CHERRY TOMATO AND BUTTER BEAN STEW

Serves 2–4

This dish can also be eaten cold as a salad.

Ingredients

- *3 tbsp olive oil*
- *1 large onion, finely chopped*
- *3 cloves garlic, finely chopped*
- *500 g (1 lb 2 oz) cherry tomatoes*
- *120 ml (4 fl oz) white wine*
- *1–2 tbsp thyme leaves*
- *3 tbsp chopped parsley*
- *salt and pepper*
- *185 g (6 oz) quinoa grain, rinsed and drained*
- *2 x 400 g (14 oz) cans butter beans, rinsed and drained*
- *350 ml (12 fl oz) hot water*
- *3 tbsp chopped chives*
- *extra virgin olive oil to serve*

Heat the olive oil in a large frying pan and sauté the onion until it is soft and starts to change color. Stir in the garlic and tomatoes and cook for about 5 minutes on medium heat, stirring occasionally, until the tomatoes start to soften. Add the wine and deglaze the pan. Stir in the thyme and parsley and season with salt and pepper.

Add the quinoa to the pan with the beans and water. Bring to the boil, then reduce the heat, cover and simmer for 10–15 minutes, until quinoa is cooked.

Stir in the chives and serve with a good drizzle of extra virgin olive oil.

CHILI BEANS

Serves 4

To make this dish vegan, use a non-dairy yogurt or sour cream. This is also great if you use it as a filling for tacos or burritos. Try it with some guacamole or tomato salsa.

Ingredients

- *2 tbsps extra virgin olive oil*
- *1 large red onion, chopped*
- *3 cloves garlic, chopped*
- *2 tsps ground sweet paprika*
- *2 tsps ground oregano*
- *1½ tbsps ground cumin*
- *½–1 tsp dried chili flakes*
- *1 x 400 g (14 oz) can diced tomatoes*
- *275 g (10 oz) quinoa, rinsed and drained*
- *590 ml (20 fl oz) boiling water*
- *pinch of salt*
- *2 x 400 g (14 oz) cans red kidney beans, rinsed*
- *20 g (¾ oz) chopped cilantro (coriander) leaves*
- *lime juice*
- *sour cream or natural Greek yogurt, for serving*

Method

Heat the oil in a large frying pan and sauté onion until soft and golden. Add the garlic and cook for about 30 seconds until fragrant. Stir in the paprika, oregano, cumin and chili flakes.

Add the tomatoes, and cover and simmer on low heat for about 5 minutes.

Stir in the quinoa, water and salt. Bring to the boil, reduce the heat, cover and simmer for 15 minutes.

Add the beans and cook for another 5–10 minutes until the beans have heated through and the quinoa is cooked.

Stir in the fresh cilantro and it is ready to serve with a squeeze of lime juice and a dollop of sour cream or yogurt.

GARBANZO BEAN AND SPINACH PILAF

Serves 4

Ingredients

- *275 g (10 oz) quinoa, rinsed and drained*
- *700 ml (24 fl oz) vegetable or chicken stock*
- *2 tbsps olive oil*
- *1 large onion, cut in half and sliced*
- *2 cloves garlic, finely chopped*
- *1 red chili, de-seeded and chopped*
- *1½–2 tsps curry powder*
- *1 tsp garam masala*
- *2 x 400 g (14 oz) cans garbanzo beans/ chickpeas, drained*
- *200 g (7 oz) fresh spinach leaves or 250 g (9 oz) frozen, thawed*
- *120 ml (4 fl oz) water*
- *juice of half a large lemon*
- *salt and freshly ground black pepper*
- *natural Greek yogurt, for serving*

Method

Place the quinoa in a small saucepan with the stock and bring to the boil. Reduce the heat, cover and simmer for 10 minutes until all the water is absorbed. Leave covered until needed.

While the quinoa is cooking, heat the oil in a large frying pan and sauté onion until soft and golden. Add the garlic and chili and cook for about 30 seconds. Stir in the curry powder and the garam masala and cook for a few seconds.

Add the garbanzo beans and the water, and simmer covered for about 5 minutes. Stir in the spinach and cook until it wilts. If using the frozen spinach, you may need to cook it for about 10 minutes and add a little more water.

Stir in the cooked quinoa, lemon juice and season with salt and pepper and mix well to combine. Serve with a dollop of yogurt.

TOMATO AND BASIL BAKED PEPPERS

Serves 2 as a main dish, 4 as entree

Cut a very fine slice off the bottom of each pepper if they do not sit straight on the baking dish. Just be careful not to cut right through.

Ingredients

- *90 g (3½ oz) quinoa grain, rinsed and drained*
- *240 ml (8 fl oz) water*
- *2 large red peppers (capsicums)*
- *250 g (8 oz) cherry tomatoes, halved*
- *2 cloves garlic, finely chopped*
- *20 g (¾ oz) chopped basil leaves*
- *2 tbsp capers*
- *2 tbsp balsamic vinegar, plus extra for serving*
- *5 tbsp extra virgin olive oil, plus extra for serving*
- *sea salt and freshly ground black pepper*

Method

Preheat the oven to 180°C (350°F).

Place the quinoa in a small saucepan with the water, bring to the boil, then reduce the heat, cover and simmer for 10 minutes until all the water is absorbed. Remove from the heat and cool completely.

Cut the peppers in half lengthways, leaving the stalks intact, and remove the seeds and excess membrane. Place on a baking tray.

For the filling, place quinoa in a large bowl with the remaining ingredients and mix well. Pile the filling into the peppers and bake for 20–30 minutes, until the peppers are soft and tender.

Drizzle with a little balsamic vinegar and extra virgin olive oil before serving. Can be eaten warm or cold.

SPINACH, MUSHROOM AND CHICKPEA CURRY

Serves 4

This is one of our favorite vegetarian family meals.

Ingredients

- *3 tbsp olive oil*
- *1 cinnamon stick*
- *1 tbsp cumin seeds*
- *1 tbsp ground turmeric*
- *1 tbsp ground cilantro (coriander)*
- *1 tbsp ground cumin*
- *2 red onion, chopped*
- *2 long green chilies, seeded and chopped*
- *350 g (12½ oz) mushrooms, sliced*
- *4 cloves garlic, chopped*
- *1 x 400 g (14 oz) can diced tomatoes*
- *140 g (5 oz) quinoa grain, rinsed and drained*
- *350 ml (12 fl oz) hot water*
- *2 x 400 g (14 oz) cans chickpeas, drained*
- *salt to taste*
- *150 g (5 oz) baby spinach leaves*
- *20 g (¾ oz) cilantro (coriander)*
- *lime juice to taste*
- *Greek yogurt for serving*

Method

Heat the olive oil in a large saucepan, stir in the cinnamon and cumin seeds and cook a few seconds until fragrant. Stir in turmeric, cilantro and cumin and cook a few seconds more to release their flavors. Add a little more oil if needed.

Add the onion and chilies and cook until the onion is soft. Stir in the mushrooms and garlic and cook for 3–4 minutes until the mushrooms soften and collapse. Add the tomatoes, stir well and bring up to a light boil. Stir in the quinoa and water, cover and simmer on low heat for 10 minutes.

Add the chickpeas, season with salt, cover and simmer for another 5–10 minutes until the quinoa is cooked and tender. Stir in the spinach and cilantro and cook until the spinach has wilted. Serve with a squeeze of lime juice and a dollop of yogurt.

RATATOUILLE

Serves 4

This is one of those dishes that is a meal on its own and you can add or substitute the vegetables above with whatever other vegetables you prefer.

Ingredients

- *1 large eggplant (aubergine)*
- *4 tbsp extra virgin olive oil*
- *1 large brown onion, chopped*
- *2 medium zucchini (courgettes), diced*
- *1 large red pepper (capsicum), seeded and chopped*
- *4 cloves garlic, finely chopped*
- *1 x 400 g (14 oz) can diced tomatoes*
- *salt and freshly ground black pepper*
- *140 g (5 oz) quinoa grain, rinsed and drained*
- *240 ml (8 fl oz) hot water*
- *a small handful chopped flatleaf parsley (optional)*

Preheat the oven to 170°C (325°F) and line a baking tray with baking paper.

Cut the eggplant into thick slices lengthways and cube. Drizzle and coat with 2 tbsp olive oil, place on the baking tray and bake in the heated oven for about 20 minutes, turning over once, until browned. Remove from the oven and set aside.

Meanwhile, heat the remaining olive oil in a large saucepan and cook the onion until soft and golden. Add the zucchini and pepper and cook for about 5 minutes, until the vegetables start to go golden. Stir in the garlic and tomatoes and season with salt and pepper. Cover and simmer for 15 minutes.

Add the quinoa to the pan with the water. Stir and simmer, covered, for 15 minutes, then add the eggplant and cook for a further 5 minutes. Stir in the parsley and serve.

STUFFED TOMATOES

Serves 4–6

When buying the tomatoes choose ones that are ripe but firm and will balance and sit upright in a baking dish. If they don't sit upright, cut a paper-thin slice off the bottom of each one and that will help them balance better.

Ingredients

- *12 large tomatoes*
- *1 tbsp ghee*
- *1 medium brown onion, chopped*
- *4 scallions (spring onions), chopped*
- *2 cloves garlic, finely chopped*
- *2 tsps curry powder*
- *1 tsp ground turmeric*
- *1 tsp ground cumin*
- *110 g (4 oz) currants*
- *225 g (8 oz) quinoa, rinsed and drained*
- *480 ml (16 fl oz) hot water*
- *Salt and freshly cracked black pepper*
- *3 tbsps chopped cilantro (coriander)*
- *extra virgin olive oil, for serving*

Cut a slice off the top of each tomato to use as a lid. Using a tsp, gently scoop out the pulp. Strain the juices from the pulp and chop the fleshy part and reserve. Discard the seeds. Invert the tomatoes onto some kitchen paper to drain off any excess moisture while you prepare the filling.

Melt the ghee in a large frying pan and sauté onion and scallions until soft and start to change color. Stir in the garlic and cook for about 30 seconds, then stir in the curry powder, turmeric and cumin, and cook for about 1 minute.

Add the currants, quinoa and water then season well with salt and pepper. Bring to the boil, reduce the heat, cover and simmer for about 15 minutes until all the water is absorbed. Cool slightly then stir in the cilantro.

Preheat oven to 180°C (350°F). Fill each tomato with the quinoa mixture, cover with the lids and place in a baking dish. Scatter the reserved tomato pulp around the tomatoes and drizzle the whole dish with extra virgin olive oil. Bake for 20–25 minutes until the tomatoes are cooked. Don't worry if the tomatoes split a little while cooking.

MANGO, SWEET POTATO AND TOMATO CURRY

Serves 6

I have used tinned mangoes so that you can prepare this lovely curry all year round. If in season use two fresh mangoes instead.

Ingredients

- *2 tbsp olive oil*
- *1 tbsp black mustard seeds*
- *1 large onion, halved and thinly sliced*
- *1 tbsp ground turmeric*
- *2 tbsp curry powder*
- *5 cardamom pods, lightly crushed*
- *a small handful fresh curry leaves*
- *4 cloves garlic, chopped*
- *1 tbsp grated fresh ginger*
- *1 long red or green chili, deseeded and sliced*
- *2 x 400 g (14 oz) cans cherry tomatoes, with juice*
- *1 x 400 g (14 oz) can coconut milk*
- *500 g (1 lb 2 oz) orange sweet potato, peeled and cubed*
- *185 g (6 oz) quinoa grain, rinsed and drained*
- *120 ml (4 fl oz) hot water*
- *1 x 800 g (26 oz) can mangoes in natural juice, drained*
- *20 g (¾ oz) chopped cilantro (coriander)*
- *lime juice for serving*

Method

Heat the oil in a large saucepan, add the mustard seeds and cook until they start to pop. Add the onion and cook until it softens. Stir in the turmeric, curry powder, cardamom and curry leaves and cook for a few seconds. Add the garlic, ginger, chili and salt and cook for a few seconds more, until fragrant.

Stir in the tomatoes, coconut milk and sweet potato, bring to the boil, then reduce heat and simmer, covered, for about 10 minutes, until the potato begins to soften. Stir in the quinoa and water and simmer on low heat for a further 15–20 minutes, until both the potato and quinoa are cooked.

Cut the mangoes into pieces, add to the pan and heat through. Stir in the cilantro, squeeze over some lime juice and serve garnished with extra cilantro leaves.

MOROCCAN PUMPKIN HALVES

Serves 4–6

I love the look of these on a platter—they look and taste very special.

Ingredients

- *1 whole butternut pumpkin, about 2 kg (4.4 lb)*
- *3½ tbsp olive oil*
- *salt and pepper*
- *45 g (1½ oz) pine nuts*
- *2 leeks, cleaned and finely sliced*
- *3 large cloves garlic*
- *1 tsp grated ginger*
- *1½ tsp ground cumin*
- *1tsp ground paprika*
- *1 tsp ground turmeric*
- *1 tsp chili flakes*
- *1 red pepper (capsicum), deseeded and chopped*
- *2 zucchini (courgettes), cubed*
- *salt and freshly ground black pepper*
- *415 ml (14 fl oz) water*
- *185 g (6 oz) quinoa grain, rinsed and drained*
- *2–3 tbsp cilantro (coriander), chopped*

Preheat the oven to 175°C (340°F).

Cut pumpkin in half lengthways and remove seeds. With a small but sturdy knife carefully remove the pumpkin flesh, creating a bowl with a border about 1.5 cm (¾ in) thick to hold the filling. Cut a very thin slice off the bottom of each pumpkin half so it will sit flat on the baking tray.

Brush the inside and edges of the pumpkin with a little olive oil and season lightly with salt and pepper. Place on a baking tray and bake for 20–25 minutes until tender.

Dry-roast the pine nuts in a small non-stick frying pan and set aside.

Heat 3 tbsp olive oil in a large frying pan and sauté the leeks until soft, add the garlic and ginger and cook for about 1 minute. Stir in the cumin, paprika, turmeric and chili, and cook for another 30 seconds. Add the pepper, zucchini, salt, pepper and 240 ml (8 fl oz) of water. Stir and simmer, covered, for 10 minutes.

Add the quinoa to the pan with 175 ml (6 fl oz) of water. Cover and simmer for another 10–12 minutes. Stir in the cilantro and toasted pine nuts. Spoon the mixture into the pumpkin halves. Return to the oven and bake for 10–15 minutes.

CREAMY LEEK AND ASPARAGUS 'QUINOTTO'

Serves 4–6

This is a quinoa version of risotto. The only difference is that the stock is added all at once and you don't have to stir constantly. The other great thing about this recipe is that you don't have to serve it immediately as you do the traditional risotto. That, to me, is an added bonus as we all know how painful it can be to round everyone up to the dinner table at the same time.

Ingredients

- *2 tbsps olive oil*
- *1 tbsp butter*
- *1 onion, chopped*
- *2 leeks, trimmed, washed and thinly sliced*
- *3 cloves garlic, grated*
- *185 g (6 oz) white quinoa, rinsed and drained*
- *185 g (6 oz) red quinoa, rinsed and drained*
- *950 ml (32 fl oz) hot vegetable stock*
- *salt and freshly cracked pepper*
- *3 bunches asparagus, trimmed and sliced*
- *2–3 tbsps cream*
- *1 tsp butter, extra*
- *90 g (3½ oz) grated parmesan*

Method

Heat the oil and melt the butter in a large saucepan. Add the onion and leeks and sauté until soft. Use as much of the green tender parts of the leeks as you can.

Stir in the garlic and cook for about a minute then add the white and red quinoa with the stock. Season with salt and pepper to taste, keeping in mind that the parmesan cheese and stock, if you are using store-bought, can be salty.

Stir well, bring to the boil, reduce the heat, cover and simmer for about 10 minutes, then stir in the asparagus excluding the tips (these are added toward the end of the cooking time). If you think of it, give the pot a stir once or twice while it is cooking.

Simmer for another 10 minutes then stir in the asparagus tips with the cream and cook for about 5–8 minutes until the quinoa is soft and almost porridgy and nearly all the liquid is absorbed.

Stir in the extra butter and parmesan, and leave to stand covered for about 10 minutes before serving.

MEXICAN CORN AND CHILI

Serves 4

This is one of those dishes that is really quick to prepare. You can have it either as a meal on its own or as an accompaniment. You can use frozen corn instead of fresh. There is no need to defrost the corn—just throw it in the pan straight from the freezer. If you use canned corn, stir it in with quinoa at the end.

Ingredients

- *275 g (10 oz) tri-color quinoa, rinsed and drained*
- *700 ml (24 fl oz) water*
- *2–3 tbsps olive oil*
- *1 large red onion, chopped*
- *1–2 red chilies, sliced*
- *3 cloves garlic, chopped*
- *600 g (21 oz) sweet corn kernels*
- *1 tsp ground allspice*
- *30 g (1 oz) chopped mint*
- *30 g (1 oz) chopped cilantro (coriander) leaves*
- *juice of 2 limes*
- *salt*
- *natural Greek yogurt or sour cream for serving*
- *chili powder, for garnish*

Place the quinoa in a small saucepan with the water and bring to the boil. Reduce the heat and simmer, covered, for 12–15 minutes until all the water is absorbed. Cover and leave to stand covered while you prepare the rest of the dish.

Heat the oil in a large frying pan and sauté the onion until soft and golden. Stir in the chili, garlic, corn and allspice, and cook until corn is tender, stirring regularly.

Add the mint, cilantro and lime juice, then season with salt. Stir in the quinoa and mix well to thoroughly combine.

Serve with a dollop of yogurt or sour cream and a sprinkle of chili powder.

CAULIFLOWER PATTIES

Makes about 15–18

Apart from being a family favorite, I have to say these patties are one of my absolute favorite vegetable dishes. I make them on a regular basis, especially in winter when the cauliflowers are at their best. I find this is also a great way to get kids to eat cauliflower as they love them. These patties are lovely served with a chutney or a sweet chili dipping sauce.

Ingredients

- *500 g (17½ oz) cauliflower florets*
- *3 scallions (spring onions), sliced*
- *2 eggs, lightly beaten*
- *2 tbs flat-leaf parsley, finely chopped*
- *1–2 cloves garlic, finely grated*
- *1 heaped tsp ground cumin*
- *salt and freshly ground black pepper*
- *60 g (2½ oz) quinoa flour*
- *olive oil, for shallow frying*

Method

Cook cauliflower in boiling salted water until quite tender. Drain well and place into a bowl to cool.

Chop the cauliflower into small pieces and then, using a fork, lightly mash. Mix in the scallions, eggs, parsley, garlic, cumin, salt and pepper. Stir in the flour and mix to combine.

Heat oil in a frying pan until medium-hot, drop spoonfuls of cauliflower into the oil and cook until golden on both sides. Remove from pan with a slotted spoon and drain on kitchen paper towels.

These are best eaten hot or warm.

SWEET POTATO AND ZUCCHINI PIE

Serves 4–6

Ingredients

- *185 g (6 oz) quinoa grain, rinsed and drained*
- *480 ml (16 fl oz) water*
- *2 tbsp olive oil*
- *1 medium onion, finely chopped*
- *2 cloves garlic, finely chopped*
- *400 g (14 oz) zucchini (courgette), coarsely grated*
- *500 g (1 lb 2 oz) orange sweet potato, cooked and mashed*
- *4 eggs*
- *120 g (4½ oz) grated tasty cheese*
- *salt and pepper*
- *1–2 tomatoes, thickly sliced*

Preheat the oven to 180°C (350°F).

Place quinoa in a small saucepan with the water. Bring to the boil, reduce the heat and simmer for 10 minutes until all the water is absorbed.

Heat the oil in a small frying pan and sauté the onion until soft and golden, then place in a large bowl. Add the cooked quinoa, garlic, zucchini, sweet potato, lightly beaten eggs, cheese, salt and pepper and mix to thoroughly combine.

Pour the mixture into a greased ovenproof dish and arrange the slices of tomato on top. Bake for 30–40 minutes until the pie is set and browned on the top.

MOZZARELLA AND ROASTED PEPPER STUFFED MUSHROOMS

Serves 4

Ingredients

- *150 g (5 oz) of quinoa, rinsed and drained*
- *350 ml (12 fl oz) water*
- *12 large mushrooms*
- *1 tbsp extra virgin olive oil*
- *4 scallions (spring onions), finely chopped*
- *2 cloves garlic, finely chopped*
- *2 tbsps finely chopped flatleaf parsley*
- *200 g (7 oz) roasted bell peppers (capsicums), chopped*
- *200 g (7 oz) mozzarella cheese, cut into small pieces*
- *1 tbsp grated parmesan cheese plus extra for sprinkling*
- *Salt and freshly cracked black pepper*

DRESSING

- *3 tbsps extra virgin olive oil*
- *2 tbsps balsamic vinegar*
- *salt and freshly cracked black pepper*

Method

Place the quinoa in a small saucepan with the water and bring to the boil. Reduce the heat, cover and simmer for 10 minutes until all the water is absorbed and the quinoa is cooked. Cool a little.

Gently wipe over the mushrooms and remove the stalk. Put 8 of the mushrooms aside and finely chop the remaining mushrooms including all of the stalks if they are not too woody or tough.

Preheat oven to 190°C (375°F) and line a baking tray with baking paper. Heat oil in a non-stick frying pan and sauté the scallions until lightly browned. Add the chopped mushrooms and cook for 3–4 minutes until the mushrooms collapse. Stir in garlic and parsley, cook for 1 minute, remove from the heat and cool. When cooled, stir in the quinoa, roasted bell peppers, mozzarella and parmesan cheeses, and season.

Place mushrooms top side down onto the tray, cover the underside of each mushroom with some of the filling squashing it down tightly as you fill it. Drizzle olive oil and sprinkle with extra parmesan cheese. Bake for about 15 minutes until the cheeses have melted. To make the dressing, mix all the ingredients together. Drizzle the mushrooms with some of the dressing before serving.

SPINACH AND GOAT'S CHEESE TART

Serves 4-6

This tart is best eaten on the day it is prepared. Quinoa flour tastes different to normal wheaten flour and can have an earthy aftertaste, which seems to be more noticeable the day after first baking. Also pastry made solely out of quinoa flour will be darker before and after baking. It is always best to re-heat this in the oven.

Ingredients

PASTRY

- *200 g (7 oz) quinoa flour*
- *1 tsp salt*
- *125 g (4 oz) very cold butter, cut into pieces*
- *2 extra large egg yolks*
- *icy cold water*
- *1 egg white, lightly beaten*

FILLING

- *1–2 tbsps extra virgin olive oil*
- *4 spring onions (scallions), chopped*
- *2 x 250 g (9 oz) packets frozen spinach, thawed*
- *1 large clove garlic, finely chopped*
- *125 g (4 oz) goat's cheese or feta*
- *2 extra large eggs*
- *240 ml (8 fl oz) cream*
- *180 ml (6 fl oz) milk*
- *salt and freshly cracked black pepper*

Place the flour and salt in a food processor and pulse for a few seconds to aerate the flour, then add the butter piece by piece and pulse until the mixture resembles thick breadcrumbs.

Add the egg yolks, process a few seconds and then, with the motor running, add as much water as needed, a little at a time until the dough comes together and turns into a ball.

Place onto a bench/counter top that has been dusted with quinoa flour and shape into a flat disc. Wrap in plastic wrap and refrigerate for about 1 hour.

Preheat oven to 180°C (350°F) and lightly grease a 25 cm (10 in) fluted tart tin with a loose base.

Remove the pastry from the fridge and roll out on a floured surface to fit the prepared tin. Gently collect the pastry by rolling around the rolling pin then gently lift it over and onto the tin. The pastry will be quite fragile so you may need to do a little repair work by pushing pastry into place in the tin. Also the pastry may have some little white specs on it after it has rested in the refrigerator, they are nothing to worry about.

Trim any excess pastry then line the tart with a piece of baking parchment/ paper and fill with baking weights.

SPINACH AND GOAT'S CHEESE TART CONTINUED

Place the tart tin on a baking tray and place in the oven to bake for 15 minutes, remove from the oven, then slowly and very carefully remove the paper and the weights. Brush the tart with some of the beaten egg white and return to the oven for another 5 minutes (this seals the inside of the tart and avoids any leakage of the custard).

In the meantime, prepare the filling by heating the oil in a medium-sized frying pan and sauté the scallions until they start to soften and take on some colour. Squeeze as much of the water as possible from the spinach then add to the pan and cook for about 3 minutes. Stir in the garlic and cook for another 1–2 minutes and remove from the heat.

Scatter the spinach over the tart and crumble the cheese on top.

Whisk together the eggs, cream and milk, and season with salt and pepper (keep in mind that the cheese can be salty).

Carefully pour the milk mixture over the spinach and cheese and bake for about 30–35 minutes until the tart is set. Remove from oven and rest for about 10 minutes before cutting and serving.

ZUCCHINI AND OLIVE BAKE

Serves 2–4

Ingredients

- *90 g (3½ oz) quinoa grain, rinsed and drained*
- *240 ml (8 fl oz) water*
- *4 scallions (spring onions), sliced*
- *1 red onion, finely chopped*
- *18 black kalamata olives, pitted and chopped*
- *1 red pepper (capsicum), seeded and chopped*
- *2 medium zucchini (courgettes), coarsely grated*
- *2 large eggs*
- *1 tsp dried oregano*
- *salt and freshly ground black pepper*

Preheat the oven to 170°C (325°F). Lightly oil a shallow baking dish.

Place the quinoa in a small saucepan with the water. Bring to the boil, then reduce the heat and simmer for 10 minutes until all the water is absorbed. Remove from the heat and cool slightly.

Place quinoa in a large bowl with all other ingredients and mix to combine. Spoon in the mixture into the baking dish and bake for about 20–30 minutes, until set and golden on top.

Allow to stand for 5–10 minutes before serving.

SPINACH AND TOMATO 'RISOTTO'

Serves 4

My family loves this served with a sprinkling of lemon juice. We don't always have it with parmesan but always with lemon juice.

Ingredients

- *3 tbsp extra virgin olive oil*
- *1 medium onion, finely chopped*
- *1 tbsp tomato paste*
- *1 x 400 g (14 oz) can diced tomatoes, with juice*
- *185 g (6 oz) quinoa grain, rinsed and drained*
- *480 ml (16 fl oz) hot water*
- *salt and freshly ground black pepper*
- *350 g (12½ oz) fresh baby spinach leaves, washed*
- *shaved parmesan cheese (optional)*

Heat the olive oil in a saucepan and cook the onions until soft and lightly browned. Stir in tomato paste and cook for 1 minute. Add the tomatoes with their juice, cover and cook on a low simmer for about 5 minutes.

Add the quinoa and hot water to the saucepan, season with salt and pepper, bring to the boil, then reduce the heat, cover and simmer for about 15 minutes. Stir in the spinach and cook for a further 3–5 minutes.

Serve immediately, with some shaved parmesan cheese if using.

BROCCOLI AND CAULIFLOWER PANAGRATTATO

Serves 4–6

This is an Italian way of preparing broccoli and cauliflower. Panagrattato means 'grated bread'—in other words, breadcrumbs. I have used quinoa flakes instead for a delicious dish that you can eat on its own or as a side dish.

Ingredients

- *500 g (1 lb 2 oz) cauliflower*
- *500 g (1 lb 2 oz) broccoli*
- *6 tbsp extra virgin olive oil, plus extra for serving*
- *6 cloves garlic, sliced*
- *4 scallions (spring onions), sliced*
- *1 tsp chili flakes*
- *80 g (3 oz) quinoa flakes*
- *salt and freshly ground black pepper to taste*
- *juice of 1 lemon*

Method

Cut the cauliflower and broccoli into florets and cook in boiling salted water until just tender but still quite crisp. Do not overcook. Drain but keep some of the cooking water.

Heat the olive oil in a large frying pan and cook the garlic, shallots and chili for 2–4 minutes until soft and just starting to change color. Stir the quinoa flakes into the garlic and shallots and cook for 2–3 minutes until the quinoa starts to toast. Add a little extra oil if the mixture seems dry—you want the flakes to cook and take on some color.

Add the cooked vegetables and a little of their cooking water; toss well to combine. Season with salt, squeeze over the lemon juice and serve with an extra drizzle of extra virgin olive oil.

Meat

PARSLEY, GARLIC AND LEMON-CRUSTED LAMB

Serves 4

The number of cutlets you prepare and serve is up to you. I usually like to serve three to four cutlets per person depending on the appetites at the table.

Ingredients

- *80 g (3 oz) parsley, chopped*
- *3 cloves garlic*
- *zest of 2 lemons*
- *2 tbsp lemon juice*
- *1 tsp extra virgin olive oil*
- *80 g (3 oz) quinoa flakes*
- *salt and freshly cracked pepper*
- *2 racks of lamb made up of*
- *6–8 frenched lamb cutlets each*
- *extra virgin olive oil, extra*
- *salt and freshly cracked black pepper, extra*

Preheat oven to 200°C (400°F) and line a baking tray with non-stick baking paper.

Place parsley, garlic, lemon zest, juice and oil in a food processor and process using the pulse setting until all the ingredients are finely chopped.

Add the quinoa flakes, salt and pepper and process for a few seconds until everything is combined and resembles a paste.

Trim lamb of any excess fat and place on the baking tray, rub with a little extra virgin olive oil and season with salt and pepper. Place in the oven and roast for 10 minutes only.

After 10 minutes, remove lamb from oven and coat with the parsley mixture pressing it down firmly.

Return lamb to the oven and roast for about 20 minutes until the lamb is cooked medium-well and the topping is golden. Lamb should be slightly pink inside but adjust cooking time as per your preference.

Remove from the oven, cover with foil, and leave to rest for a good 10 minutes before slicing and serving.

BACON MEAT LOAF

Serves 6

This is a family favorite among the men in my family and it goes such a long way. Leftover meat loaf sandwiches are just the best. If you are sensitive to gluten/wheat, omit the Worcestershire sauce.

Ingredients

- *750 g (1 lb 10 oz) minced beef*
- *1 medium onion, coarsely grated*
- *1 medium carrot, coarsely grated*
- *3 cloves garlic, finely grated*
- *100 g (3½ oz) frozen peas, thawed*
- *60 g (2½ oz) quinoa flakes*
- *2 tsp dried oregano leaves*
- *60 ml (2 fl oz) tomato sauce/ketchup*
- *1 tbsp Worcestershire sauce*
- *2 eggs*
- *3 tbsp chopped flatleaf parsley*
- *salt and freshly ground black pepper*
- *5–6 rashers of bacon*

Method

Preheat the oven to 175°C (340°F).

Place the mince in a large bowl with all the other ingredients except for the bacon and mix thoroughly.

Lightly oil a large loaf tin and line with the bacon slices—place them, side by side, across the bottom of the tin, letting them overhang the sides of the tin. Spoon the meatloaf mixture on top of the bacon and level the top. Fold the overhanging bacon rashers over the meatloaf to enclose.

Bake in the oven for about 1–1½ hours, until cooked and browned. If the top is browning too quickly cover with foil. Rest for 10–15 minutes before slicing.

SPICY ITALIAN SAUSAGES WITH PEPPERS AND FENNEL

Serves 4-6

If you are gluten/wheat intolerant, be aware that some sausages are made with breadcrumbs and/or cereal.

Ingredients

- *275 g (10 oz) quinoa, rinsed and drained*
- *700 ml (24 fl oz) water*
- *1 kg (2 lb 4 oz) spicy Italian sausages*
- *2 bulbs baby fennel*
- *2 tbsps extra virgin olive oil*
- *1 large onion, halved then sliced*
- *3 cloves garlic, sliced*
- *1 red bell pepper (capsicum), cut into pieces*
- *1 green bell pepper (capsicum), cut into pieces*
- *1 tsp fennel seeds*
- *½–1 tsp chili flakes*
- *Salt and freshly cracked pepper*
- *Juice ½–1 lemon (optional)*

Method

Place the quinoa in a medium-sized saucepan with the water, bring to the boil, cover, reduce the heat and simmer for 10 minutes until all the water is absorbed. Remove from the heat and leave to stand, covered.

Remove the sausage meat from the casings. Discard the casings. Roll the meat into little balls and set aside in the fridge. Cut the fennel bulbs in half and thickly slice. Reserve any of the green fronds as they will be used to garnish the dish. Heat the oil in a large frying pan and cook the meatballs until browned and cooked, remove from the pan and put to one side.

Add the onion to the pan and sauté until soft and golden. You may need to add a little more oil. Add the fennel to the onions with the garlic, peppers, fennel seeds and chili and cook until the vegetables take on some color and are tender but still firm. Return the meat to the pan and season with salt and pepper then stir in the quinoa and lemon juice if using. Gently mix together until the quinoa has combined with all the other ingredients. Check and adjust the seasoning if necessary and cook on a low heat for about 5 minutes to heat everything through. Garnish with the fennel fronds and serve.

BEEF LASAGNE

Serves 4–6

You can make this lasagne using lasagne sheets made out of the basic pasta dough recipe found in the Breads and Pasta chapter of this book.

Ingredients

- *275 g (10 oz) quinoa grain, rinsed and drained*
- *700 ml (24 fl oz) water*
- *1 tbsp olive oil*

MINCE SAUCE

- *2 tbsp olive oil*
- *1 large brown onion, finely chopped*
- *500 g (1 lb 2 oz) beef mince*
- *3 cloves garlic, finely chopped*
- *3 tbsp tomato paste*
- *1 tsp dried oregano*
- *1 x 400 g (14 oz) can diced tomatoes, with juice*
- *salt and freshly ground black pepper*
- *480 ml (16 fl oz) water*

CHEESE SAUCE

- *4 tbsp butter*
- *6 tbsp quinoa flour*
- *830 ml (28 fl oz) milk*
- *90 g (3½ oz) grated tasty cheese*
- *45 g (1½ oz) grated parmesan cheese*

Preheat the oven to 185°C (360°F). Place the quinoa and water in a pan, bring to boil, reduce heat, cover and simmer for 10 minutes.

For the mince sauce, heat oil, add onion and sauté until golden. Add the mince and cook until it browns. Stir in the garlic, cook for 1 minute, then add tomato paste and cook for 1–2 minutes. Add oregano, tomatoes with juice, salt and pepper and water. Bring to the boil, then reduce the heat, cover with the lid slightly ajar, and simmer for 30–35 minutes until cooked and thick but not dry.

For the cheese sauce, melt butter, stir in flour and cook for a few seconds until the butter and flour are well incorporated and a roux is formed. Slowly pour in the milk and whisk continuously until the sauce thickens and starts to bubble. Stir in the cheese. Check for saltiness before seasoning.

Place the quinoa in a large bowl, stir through the olive oil and season.

Spread a thin layer of the cheese sauce on the bottom of a baking dish, add a third of the quinoa; flatten and top with a thin layer of cheese sauce and half the mince sauce. Repeat the layering, ending with quinoa and sauce. Sprinkle with extra parmesan cheese and bake for 30–40 minutes, until golden brown. Allow to stand for at least 30 minutes before serving.

CHORIZO SAUSAGE WITH CARAMELIZED ONIONS AND SMOKED PAPRIKA

Serves 4

Ingredients

- *275 g (10 oz) quinoa, rinsed and drained*
- *700 ml (24 fl oz) water*
- *4 chorizo sausages, thickly sliced*
- *1 tbsp extra virgin olive oil*
- *2 large onions, halved then sliced*
- *2 cloves garlic, chopped*
- *½–1 tsp chili flakes*
- *2 tsps smoked paprika*
- *60 g (2½ oz) frozen peas*
- *60 ml (2 fl oz) water*
- *salt and freshly cracked black pepper*
- *2 tbsps chopped parsley, for serving*

Method

Place the quinoa in a small to medium saucepan with the water, bring to the boil, then reduce the heat, cover and simmer for 10 minutes or until all the water is absorbed. Remove from heat.

Sauté chorizo in a large, non-stick frying pan until lightly browned (there is no need to add any oil to the pan at this stage as the chorizo should render some of its own fat). Remove the chorizo from the pan with a slotted spoon and set aside.

Add the oil to the pan if necessary and cook the onion, stirring regularly until soft and caramelized, for about 5 minutes. Stir in the garlic and chili flakes and cook for about 30 seconds, then stir in the chili and paprika.

Add the frozen peas and water, and cook for about 4–5 minutes, stirring frequently until peas have thawed and are just cooked.

Stir in the quinoa and the chorizo sausage, season with salt and pepper, and cook for another 3–4 minutes until heated through. Sprinkle with parsley and serve.

INDIVIDUAL EGGPLANT MOUSSAKA

Serves 2–4

With a Greek heritage, is it any wonder that moussaka is one of my favorite meals? These individual servings are great for a dinner party or serve half as an entrée. Lamb mince can be substituted for the beef. Serve with a Greek salad.

Ingredients

- *2 large eggplants (aubergines)*
- *extra virgin olive oil*
- *1–2 tbsp olive oil*
- *450 g (1 lb) beef mince*
- *1 onion, finely chopped*
- *2 cloves garlic, finely chopped*
- *2 tbsp tomato paste*
- *1x 400 g (14 oz) can diced tomatoes*
- *1 tsp ground cinnamon*
- *240 ml (8 fl oz) water, plus 175 ml (2½ fl oz)*
- *salt and pepper to taste*
- *90 g (3½ oz) quinoa grain, rinsed and drained*

WHITE SAUCE

- *1 tbsp butter*
- *1 tbsp quinoa flour*
- *240 ml (8 fl oz) milk*
- *1 tsp grated parmesan cheese*

Method

Preheat the oven to 170°C (340°F). Cut the eggplants in half lengthways, keeping the stalk intact. Trim a fine slice off the bottom of each half. Scoop out and reserve as much pulp as possible, leaving a firm but not too thick shell. Brush all over with extra virgin olive oil and place on a lined baking tray. Bake for about 20 minutes, until tender.

Heat 1–2 tbsp olive oil in a large frying pan and brown the mince, then add the onion and garlic and cook 2–4 minutes, until the onion is soft. Roughly chop the reserved eggplant pulp and stir it into the mince. Add the tomato paste and cook for 1–2 minutes, then add the tomatoes, cinnamon, water, salt and pepper, and simmer for 10 minutes.

Stir in the quinoa and extra water and simmer, covered, on low heat for another 15–20 minutes, stirring occasionally. Cool slightly.

For the sauce, melt the butter in a saucepan and stir in the flour. Slowly pour in the milk, stirring until it starts to bubble. Stir in cheese and pepper and cook until the sauce thickens.

Fill each eggplant with mince, cover with sauce and sprinkle with cinnamon and parmesan. Bake for 20–30 minutes until golden.

STEAK WITH MUSHROOM GRAVY

Serves 4

Ingredients

- *4 steaks, T-bone, rump, sirloin or fillet*
- *extra virgin olive oil*
- *salt and pepper*

MUSHROOM GRAVY

- *250 g (4 oz) button mushrooms, finely sliced*
- *extra virgin olive oil, extra*
- *1–2 cloves garlic, finely chopped*
- *2 tbsp quinoa flour*
- *120 ml (4 fl oz) white wine*
- *240 ml (8 fl oz) beef or chicken stock*
- *2 tbsp flat-leaf parsley, finely chopped*
- *salt and freshly cracked black pepper*

Have the steak at room temperature and rub the oil, salt and pepper on both sides of the steak.

Heat a griddle pan or large frying pan until very hot. Add the steak (you should hear an immediate sizzle) and cook for about 3–4 minutes on each side or to your liking, then turn over again and quickly cook for about 15–20 seconds only on both sides.

When the steak is cooked to your liking remove from the pan, place on to a plate and cover tightly with foil. Allow to rest for about 5–7 minutes.

While the steak is resting, pour a little oil in the pan add the mushrooms and garlic and quickly toss on high heat until the mushrooms collapse and take on some color.

Stir in the flour then pour in the wine and deglaze the pan by allowing the alcohol to evaporate. Cook for about 1 minute.

Add the stock and parsley and season to taste. Cook for about 2–3 minutes until the mushrooms are cooked and the gravy has thickened. Pour whatever juices have come out of the steaks while resting into the gravy and stir.

Serve the steaks with the mushroom gravy.

MEAT PIE

Makes 4 pies

These pies may sound a bit fiddly to make but they are actually very easy. Keep in mind that because quinoa flour is used to make the pastry, it may not roll out as easily as pastry made with regular flour and you may need to ease the pastry into the tins. This is why I find the pastry is much easier to handle and to transfer into the tins after rolling onto non-stick paper first. After you have made them for the first time you will see they are not hard at all to make and are really worth the little extra time.

Ingredients

- *250 g (9 oz) quinoa flour*
- *½ tsp salt*
- *1 tsp baking powder*
- *125 g (4 oz) very cold unsalted butter, cut into pieces*
- *120 ml (4 fl oz) icy cold water*
- *1 egg, beaten*
- *tomato sauce, for serving*

FILLING

- *1 tbsp olive oil*
- *1 large onion, chopped*
- *450 g (16 oz) minced (ground) beef*
- *2 cloves garlic, finely chopped*
- *1 tbsp tomato paste (concentrate)*
- *1 tsp mixed herbs*
- *1 tbsp quinoa flour*
- *salt and freshly cracked pepper*
- *240 ml (8 fl oz) beef stock*
- *1 tbsp of your favorite chutney*

Place the flour, salt and baking powder in a food processor. Pulse for a few seconds to aerate the flour then add the butter and pulse until the mixture resembles fine breadcrumbs.

With the motor running, add the water a little at a time until the dough comes together and turns into a ball. Turn onto a floured surface and shape into a flat disc. Wrap in plastic wrap and refrigerate for about 1 hour.

To make the filling, heat the oil in a frying pan or saucepan and sauté onion until golden. Add the beef and cook until browned then stir in the garlic and tomato paste and cook for about 1 minute.

Continued over page...

MEAT PIE CONTINUED

Stir in the herbs and the flour, season with salt and pepper then add the stock. Bring to the boil, lower heat and simmer covered for about 5 minutes. Remove from the heat, stir in the chutney and allow to cool.

Preheat the oven to 180°C (350°F) and lightly oil four 125 ml (4 oz) individual pie tins.

Divide the pastry into four then place onto a sheet of non-stick baking paper. Cut each piece into two pieces, one to cover the base and sides of the pie tin and the other (a smaller piece) to use as a lid. Roll out the pastry and line the tins.

Divide the filling between the four pie tins. Cover the pies with a pastry lid then lightly press the edges together to seal. Cut a small vent on the top of each pie.

If you're feeling up to it, cut out some decorative shapes from any leftover pastry for the tops of the pies. Brush with beaten egg and bake for about 25–30 minutes until golden. Stand for about

10 minutes before gently removing from tins. Serve with lots of tomato sauce.

SWEET POTATO, BACON AND CHILI BAKE

Serves 6

This can be eaten hot or cold and it is ideal for lunches or to take to picnics. It is best to grate the potato just before you use it as it can discolor very quickly.

Ingredients

- *140 g (5 oz) quinoa, rinsed and drained*
- *350 ml (12 fl oz) water*
- *500 g (17½ oz) sweet potato, peeled and coarsely grated*
- *3–4 rashers bacon, rind removed, and chopped*
- *4 scallions (spring onions), sliced*
- *1 long red chili, de-seeded and chopped*
- *2 cloves garlic, finely chopped*
- *1 tsp ground turmeric*
- *4 eggs*
- *180 g (6 oz) tasty or mild cheddar cheese, grated*
- *salt and freshly ground pepper*

Method

Preheat oven to 180°C (350°F) and lightly grease a 30 x 20 cm (8 x 10 in) baking dish.

Place quinoa in a small saucepan with the water, bring to the boil, then reduce the heat, cover and simmer for about 10 minutes until all the water is absorbed. Remove from the heat and cool.

Place the quinoa in a large bowl with the potato, bacon, scallions, chili, garlic, turmeric, eggs, cheese, salt and pepper and mix well to combine.

Pour mixture into baking dish and bake for 45–50 minutes until golden and crisp. Rest for around 10 minutes before slicing.

CRUMBED LAMB CUTLETS WITH GARLIC, LEMON AND OREGANO

Serves 4–6

Ingredients

- *12 lamb cutlets*
- *80 g (3 oz) quinoa flakes*
- *2–3 cloves garlic, finely grated*
- *zest of 1 lemon*
- *2 tsp dried oregano leaves*
- *salt and freshly ground black pepper*
- *80 g (3 oz) quinoa flour*
- *2 eggs, lightly beaten*
- *olive oil for shallow-frying*
- *squeeze of lemon juice*

Trim the cutlets of any excess fat and lightly pound with a mallet to flatten.

Combine the quinoa flakes with the garlic, lemon zest, oregano, salt and pepper; set aside.

Lightly dust each cutlet with some flour, dip in the beaten egg, then press into the quinoa flake mixture and coat well.

Heat the oil in a large frying pan until hot and gently shallow-fry the cutlets on a medium heat until golden, about 2–3 minutes each side. Serve hot with a squeeze of lemon juice.

BARBECUE PORK WITH ASIAN-STYLE QUINOA

Serves 4

Ingredients

- *2 cloves garlic, grated*
- *1 tbsp grated fresh ginger*
- *¼ tsp five spice powder*
- *2–3 tbsps tamari soy sauce*
- *2 tbsps oil*
- *1 tbsp honey*
- *2 pork fillets, about 1 kg (2 lb 4 oz)*

ASIAN-STYLE QUINOA

- *275 g (10 oz) quinoa, rinsed and drained*
- *700 ml (24 fl oz) water*
- *1 stick lemongrass, bruised*
- *2 star anise*
- *1 large clove garlic, lightly smashed*
- *3–4 slices fresh ginger*
- *2 tbsps tamari soy sauce*
- *2 red chilies, left whole*
- *2 green chilies, left whole*
- *cilantro (coriander) leaves, chopped, for garnish*
- *lime juice, for garnish*

Method

Preheat the oven to 180°C (350°F).

Mix together the garlic, ginger, five spice powder, soy sauce, oil and honey. Pour over the pork and leave to marinate for 1–2 hours—the longer the better—then roast in the oven for 20–25 minutes or until cooked to your preference. Remove from the oven, cover with foil and rest for 5–10 minutes.

In the meantime, prepare the quinoa by placing it in a medium-sized saucepan with the water, lemongrass, star anise, garlic, ginger, soy sauce and chilies.

Bring to the boil, reduce the heat, cover, and simmer for 10–12 minutes until all the liquid is absorbed. Remove from the heat and leave to stand, covered, for 10–15 minutes.

Toss the cilantro through the quinoa and serve on a large platter with a good sprinkle of lime juice and with slices of the pork fillets on top.

LAMB WITH GARLIC, CUMIN AND PEAS

Serves 4

This is great served with some finely sliced red chillies and lemon wedges. A dollop of thick Greek yoghurt is very nice with it also. If you are sensitive to gluten/wheat, use a wheat-free tamari soy sauce.

Ingredients

- *2 tbsp olive oil*
- *2 medium onions*
- *500 g (1lb 2oz) minced lamb*
- *4 cloves garlic, chopped*
- *1 tsp cumin seeds*
- *1 heaped tbsp ground cumin*
- *180 g (6 oz) quinoa grain, rinsed and drained*
- *1 tbsp soy sauce*
- *chilli powder to taste*
- *salt*
- *480 ml (8 fl oz) hot water*
- *150 g (5 oz) frozen peas*
- *red chillies for serving*
- *lemon wedges for serving*

Method

Heat the olive oil in a large deep frying pan. Cut onions in half and thinly slice. Add to the pan and cook until soft and golden. Add the mince and cook until well browned. Stir in the garlic, cumin seeds and ground cumin and cook for 1–2 minutes, until fragrant.

Add the quinoa, soy sauce, chilli powder, salt and water.

Stir, cover and simmer on low heat for 10–15 minutes, until the quinoa is almost cooked.

Add a little extra water if the mixture is too dry. Stir in the frozen peas and cook for another 10 minutes.

MOROCCAN LAMB ROAST WITH YELLOW QUINOA

Serves 6

This is a family favorite in my house and is a great meal to prepare when you have guests. The cooking time for the lamb varies according to your oven but also depends on how you like your lamb.

Ingredients

- *1 tbsp cumin seeds*
- *1 tbsp cilantro (coriander) seeds*
- *½ bunch fresh cilantro (coriander), including stems and root*
- *4–5 large cloves garlic*
- *1 tsp ground paprika*
- *1 tsp ground cumin*
- *1 tsp ground turmeric*
- *½ tsp cinnamon*
- *½–1 tsp dried chili flakes*
- *2 tbsp extra virgin olive oil*
- *juice of 1 large lemon*
- *salt*
- *1 x 2 kg (4 lb 6 oz) boned leg of lamb*
- *Greek yogurt, for serving*
- *lemon juice, for serving*
- *cilantro (coriander) leaves, for serving*

YELLOW QUINOA

- *1–2 tbsp extra virgin olive oil*
- *1 tsp black mustard seeds*
- *6 scallions (spring onions), sliced*
- *7 cardamom pods*
- *1 heaped tbsp grated fresh turmeric or 2 tsp ground*
- *¼ tsp cinnamon*
- *370 g (12½ oz) quinoa, rinsed and drained*
- *salt and freshly cracked black pepper*
- *950 ml (32 fl oz) boiling water*

Dry-roast the cumin and cilantro seeds in a small non-stick frying pan until fragrant. Keep an eye on them as they can burn very easily.

Place seeds in a mortar and pestle and grind to a coarse powder.

Continued over the page...

MOROCCAN LAMB ROAST WITH YELLOW QUINOA CONTINUED

Chop the cilantro root and stems into small pieces, add to the mortar and pestle with the garlic, paprika, cumin, turmeric, cinnamon and chili and grind to a paste with the olive oil and lemon juice.

Finely chop the cilantro leaves and mix into the paste, season with salt.

Lay out the lamb onto a large roasting pan that has been lined with non-stick baking paper (this helps with the washing up later). Using a sharp knife, make some deep cuts all along the inside part of the lamb so as to open it up even more, known as a 'butterfly' cut. This not only helps the marinade penetrate the meat more but also cuts down on the cooking time.

Completely cover the lamb all over with the marinade making sure you rub it right into all the cuts. Cover and leave to marinade in the fridge for at least 4–6 hours or, preferably, overnight.

Take the lamb out of the fridge 1 hour before cooking and bring back to room temperature.

Preheat oven to 200°C (400°F) and roast the lamb for 1–1¼ hours, depending on how well done you like your lamb to be cooked. Lamb is best cooked when still slightly pink in the centre.

Remove from the oven, cover tightly with foil and rest for a good 10–15 minutes before serving with the yellow quinoa.

While the lamb is cooking, prepare the yellow quinoa. Heat oil in a large, deep frying pan and cook the mustard seeds until they start to pop. Add the scallions and sauté until they are soft.

Add the cardamom, turmeric and cinnamon and cook for about 1 minute. Stir in the quinoa, season with salt and water then pour in the water, bring back to the boil, reduce the heat to low, cover and simmer for about 15 minutes until all the liquid is absorbed.

Fluff up with a fork and serve on a large platter topped with the sliced lamb. Squeeze some extra lemon over the lamb and sprinkle with extra cilantro leaves.

Serve with a dollop of Greek yogurt.

CHILI CON CARNE

Serves 6

Ingredients

- *2 tbsps olive oil*
- *1 large onion, finely chopped*
- *500 g (17½ oz) ground/minced beef*
- *3 cloves garlic, chopped*
- *2 tbsps dried oregano*
- *2 tbsps ground cumin*
- *1 tbsp ground paprika*
- *½–1 tsp chili powder*
- *2 tbsps tomato concentrate/paste*
- *2 x 400 g (14 oz) cans diced tomatoes*
- *salt, to taste*
- *240 ml (8 fl oz) water*
- *275 g (10 oz), quinoa, rinsed and drained*
- *590 ml (20 fl oz) boiling water*
- *2 x 400 g (14 oz) cans red kidney beans, drained and rinsed*
- *Parmesan, grated, for serving*
- *cilantro (coriander), chopped, for garnish*
- *sour cream, for garnish*
- *avocado, sliced (optional)*

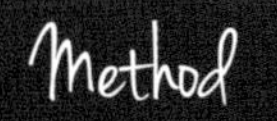

Heat the oil in a large, deep frying pan and sauté onion until soft and golden. Add the beef and continue cooking until browned, making sure any lumps are broken up.

Stir in the garlic and cook for about 30 seconds until fragrant, then add the oregano, cumin, paprika and chili and cook for about 1 minute,

Stir in tomato concentrate then add the undrained tomatoes, salt and water. Reduce heat, cover and simmer on low heat for about 15 minutes.

Stir in the quinoa and boiling water, cover and simmer for about 20 minutes, stirring occasionally until the quinoa is cooked.

Stir in the red kidney beans and simmer on low heat until the beans are heated through and all the flavors have combined (about 5 minutes).

Rest for about 10 minutes before serving with a sprinkling of grated parmesan, some fresh cilantro and a dollop of sour cream. Slices of fresh avocado are also lovely served with this chili.

LAMB WITH POMEGRANATE, MINT AND NUTS

Serves 4

Ingredients

- *185 g (6 oz) quinoa grain, rinsed and drained*
- *480 ml (16 fl oz) water*
- *750 g (1 lb 10 oz) lamb fillets*
- *2 tbsp olive oil, plus 1 tsp for the lamb*
- *60 g (2 oz) skinless almond kernels*
- *45 g (1½ oz) pine nuts*
- *150 g (5 oz) golden raisins or sultanas*
- *60 g (2 oz) pistachio nuts*
- *salt and pepper to taste*
- *1 large pomegranate*
- *30 g (1 oz) chopped mint*
- *salt and freshly ground black pepper to taste*

Method

Place the quinoa and water in a small pan. Bring to the boil, then reduce the heat and simmer, covered, for 10 minutes until all the water is absorbed. Remove from the heat and set aside.

Heat a griddle pan or frying pan until hot. Rub the lamb fillets on both sides with a little olive oil and season with salt and pepper. Place in the hot pan, sear well on both sides and cook to your liking; about 3–4 minutes on each side if you want the meat pink. Place on a plate, cover tightly with foil to keep warm and allow to rest.

Heat 2 tbsps of olive oil in a large frying pan, add the almonds and gently toast until they start to change color. Add the pine nuts and sultanas and cook for another 1–2 minutes. Keep a close eye on them as the nuts and sultanas tend to color quickly.

Stir in the cooked quinoa and pistachio nuts and mix well. Slice the lamb into thin slices and add to the pan with any meat juices left on the plate.

Cut the pomegranate in half and, with the back of a wooden spoon, bash the fruit straight out of both halves and into the pan. Give a little squeeze to release any juice. Stir in the mint, check the seasoning and serve.

CHORIZO SAUSAGE WITH PEAS AND TOMATOES

Serves 4

You can substitute shrimps or strips of chicken breast for the chorizo. If using chicken, cook it almost completely at the beginning. Shrimps can be added at the last minute but vary the cooking time accordingly.

Ingredients

- *3 chorizo sausages*
- *2 tbsp olive oil*
- *1 large onion, finely chopped*
- *3 large cloves garlic, finely chopped*
- *1 tsp sweet paprika*
- *1 x 400 g (14 oz) can cherry tomatoes, undrained*
- *370 g (12½ oz) quinoa grain, rinsed and drained*
- *700 ml (24 fl oz) hot water*
- *salt and pepper*
- *300 g (10½ oz) frozen peas*
- *3 tbsp chopped flatleaf parsley*
- *2 tbsp chopped chives*

Method

Cut the chorizo into quarters lengthways, then into pieces. Heat the oil in a large deep frying pan and cook the chorizo until golden, then remove from the pan.

Add the onion and sauté until soft, adding a little extra oil if needed. Stir in the garlic and cook until fragrant, then add the paprika, cherry tomatoes, quinoa and water. Season to taste, cover and simmer for 10 minutes. Stir in the peas, parsley, chives and chorizo and simmer, covered, for a further 8–10 minutes.

Poultry

CHICKEN MEXICANA

Serves 4

Another one-pot favorite, this is a really good meal to prepare when your children have friends over for dinner.

Ingredients

- *3 tbsp olive oil*
- *2 medium red onions, chopped*
- *800 g (28 oz) chicken thigh fillets, diced*
- *3–4 cloves garlic, chopped*
- *1 tbsp ground paprika*
- *1 tsp dried oregano leaves*
- *2 tsp ground cumin*
- *1 tsp ground chili*
- *1 red pepper (capsicum), deseeded and cut into chunks*
- *1 green pepper (capsicum), deseeded and cut into chunks*
- *1 x 400 g (14 oz) can diced tomatoes, with juice*
- *salt*
- *185 g (6 oz) quinoa grain, rinsed and drained*
- *2 x 400 g (14 oz) cans red kidney beans, rinsed and drained*
- *350 ml (12 fl oz) hot water*

GARNISH

- *1–2 avocados*
- *sour cream or Greek yogurt*
- *cilantro (coriander), chopped*

Method

Heat the olive oil in a large frying pan and sauté the onions until soft and golden. Add the chicken and cook for 3–5 minutes, until sealed all over. Stir in the garlic, paprika, oregano, cumin and chili and cook for about 30 seconds until fragrant.

Stir in the peppers, tomatoes and juice and season with salt. Reduce the heat, cover and simmer for 10 minutes. Add the quinoa to the pan with the red kidney beans and water. Stir well, bring back to a simmer, cover and cook for about 15 minutes, stirring occasionally until the quinoa and chicken are cooked.

Serve with slices of avocado, a dollop of sour cream or plain yogurt and chopped cilantro leaves.

HERB-CRUMBED CHICKEN TENDERLOINS

Serves 6

If you prefer, you can leave out the herbs or substitute other favorites. Either way, these are always a great hit and kids love them. They are good served with a Thai sweet chili sauce.

Ingredients

- *1 kg (2 lb 3 oz) chicken breast tenderloins*
- *120 g (4½ oz) quinoa flakes*
- *1 tbsp chopped thyme leaves*
- *1 tbsp chopped chives*
- *salt and freshly ground black pepper*
- *90 g (3½ oz) quinoa flour*
- *2–3 eggs, lightly beaten*
- *light olive oil for shallow-frying*

Method

Trim any fat and any bits of tendons from the tenderloins.

Combine the quinoa flakes with the herbs, salt and pepper.

Dust the tenderloins with flour, dip them in the beaten egg, then coat with the flake mixture, pressing down to make sure the tenderloins are well covered.

Heat the oil until hot and gently shallow-fry on a medium heat about 3 minutes on each side, until they are cooked through and golden brown.

CHICKEN AND LEEKS IN A CREAMY MUSTARD SAUCE WITH HERBED QUINOA

Serves 4

Ingredients

- *2 leeks*
- *2 tbsp olive oil*
- *4 half chicken breast fillets, skinned*
- *2 cloves garlic, finely chopped*
- *2 tbsp Dijon mustard*
- *175 ml (6 fl oz) white wine*
- *2 tbsp thyme leaves*
- *salt and freshly ground pepper*
- *175 ml (6 fl oz) cream*

HERBED QUINOA

- *275 g (10 oz) quinoa, rinsed and drained*
- *700 ml (24 fl oz) water*
- *2 tbsp butter*
- *2 tbsp fresh chives, chopped*
- *2 tbsp flat-leaf parsley, chopped*
- *1 tbsp fresh thyme leaves*
- *salt and freshly cracked pepper*

Method

Prepare leeks by washing and removing all dirt and grit that is normally lodged between all the layers then slice thinly, including some of the more tender green parts.

Heat oil in a large, deep frying pan until hot, add the chicken and brown on both sides. Remove from pan, cover and keep warm. Add leeks to the pan and sauté until tender, stir in garlic and cook for about 30 seconds until fragrant.

Stir in mustard, then add wine and the thyme. Return chicken to pan and cook for about 1–2 minutes until the alcohol evaporates.

Season then add the cream, stir well and bring to the boil. Reduce heat, cover and simmer for about 15 minutes until chicken is completely cooked and sauce has thickened. If sauce is too runny, cook, uncovered, for another 2 minutes or so until the sauce has thickened. Serve with herbed quinoa.

To make herbed quinoa, place quinoa in a small saucepan with the water, bring to the boil, then reduce the heat, cover and simmer for 10 minutes until all the water is absorbed. Melt the butter in a frying pan, add the herbs and cook for 1–2 minutes, stir in the cooked quinoa, season with salt and pepper and cook until heated through.

CHICKEN AND THYME PATTIES

Makes 12 patties

Ingredients

- *90 g (3½ oz) red quinoa, rinsed and drained*
- *240 ml (8 fl oz) water*
- *1 kg (2 lb 4 oz) minced (ground) chicken*
- *1 large onion, finely chopped*
- *2 cloves garlic, finely chopped*
- *1 tbsp Dijon mustard (or your favorite mustard)*
- *2 tbsp fresh thyme leaves, finely chopped*
- *1 tbsp fresh flat-leaf parsley, finely chopped*
- *1 large egg*
- *salt and freshly ground pepper*
- *40 g (1½ oz) quinoa flakes*
- *salt and freshly ground black pepper, extra*
- *1 tbsp flat-leaf parsley, finely chopped, extra*

Method

Place quinoa in a small saucepan with the water, bring to the boil, then reduce heat, cover and simmer for 10–13 minutes until all the water is absorbed. Remove from heat and cool.

Place chicken in a large mixing bowl with the cooled quinoa, onion, garlic, mustard, thyme, parsley and egg, season with salt and pepper and mix well until thoroughly combined.

Mix the quinoa flakes with the extra parsley and season with a little salt and pepper.

Divide chicken mixture into 12 and shape into large patties then lightly press into the quinoa flake mixture to coat on both sides.

Heat oil in a large frying pan until hot and fry the patties on medium heat until golden brown on both sides and cooked right through.

QUAIL WITH ARUGULA, GARLIC AND PINE NUT STUFFING

Serves 4

Ingredients

- *30 g (1 oz) pine nuts*
- *2 tbsp olive oil*
- *2 shallots (eschalots), finely chopped*
- *4 scallions (spring onions), finely sliced*
- *3 large cloves garlic, finely chopped*
- *150 g (5 oz) baby arugula (rocket), roughly chopped*
- *salt and freshly ground black pepper*
- *2 tsp balsamic vinegar*
- *40 g (1½ oz) quinoa flakes*
- *1 egg*
- *8 quails*
- *olive oil*
- *juice of 1 lemon*
- *120 ml (4 fl oz) white wine*
- *1 tsp chopped thyme leaves*
- *1 tsp chopped rosemary leaves*
- *ground paprika*

Preheat the oven to 185°C (360°F).

Lightly dry-roast the pine nuts in a small non-stick frying pan. Set aside to cool.

Heat the olive oil in a frying pan and sauté the eschalots and scallions until golden. Stir in the garlic and cook for another 30 seconds. Add the arugula, salt and pepper, stir, cover and cook on medium heat for about 2–3 minutes until the arugula wilts. Cool slightly, then mix in the balsamic vinegar, roasted pine nuts, quinoa flakes and egg.

Prepare the quails: remove any feathers, rinse under running water and pat dry. Fill each quail with the stuffing mixture and tie the bottom of the drumsticks together with kitchen string.

Place the quails into a roasting dish, rub with olive oil and pour over the lemon juice and wine. Sprinkle with thyme, rosemary and paprika and season with salt and pepper. Cover with foil and roast for 15 minutes, then remove the foil and roast for another 20–30 minutes, until the quails are golden and cooked, basting occasionally with the pan juices. Add water to the pan if the liquid dries out.

TURKEY SAUSAGES

Makes about 18 sausages

These turkey 'sausages' can be eaten hot or cold and are really nice for school lunches or picnics.

Ingredients

- *90 g (3½ oz) quinoa, rinsed and drained*
- *240 ml (8 fl oz) water*
- *500 g (17½ oz) minced (ground) turkey*
- *2 cloves garlic, finely grated*
- *1 small red onion, coarsely grated*
- *4 scallions (spring onions), very finely sliced*
- *1 long red chili, de-seeded and finely chopped (optional)*
- *1 tsp lemon zest*
- *2 tsp dried mixed herbs*
- *1 tsp sweet paprika*
- *2 extra large eggs*
- *salt and freshly ground black pepper*
- *olive oil, for shallow cooking*
- *lemon wedges, tomato sauce (ketchup) or mustard, for serving*

Place quinoa in a small saucepan with the water, bring to the boil, then reduce heat, cover and simmer for 10 minutes until all the water is absorbed. Remove from the heat and cool.

Place turkey in a bowl with the garlic, onion, scallions, chili if using, lemon zest, mixed herbs, paprika and eggs, season with salt and pepper to taste.

Add the quinoa and mix really well to combine all of the ingredients together.

Take spoonfuls of the mixture and roll with your hands to form a sausage shape.

Heat a little olive oil in a large non-stick frying pan until hot.

Add the sausages and shallow-fry on a medium heat until cooked and browned all over.

Serve with lemon wedges or tomato or mustard sauce.

FETTUCCINI WITH CHICKEN AND MUSHROOM SAUCE

Serves 4

Fresh pasta dough can be easily and successfully made with quinoa flour. The quinoa pasta is a little more delicate and requires more patience, especially when making it for the first time. But persevere—it is really worth it. The pasta does not take very long to cook and can be a little darker in color once cooked.

Ingredients

- *3 tbsps extra virgin olive oil*
- *750 g (26 oz) chicken fillet, cut into strips*
- *4 scallions (spring onions), sliced*
- *4 cloves garlic, finely chopped*
- *400 g (14 oz) mushrooms, thinly sliced*
- *300 ml (10 fl oz) cream*
- *175 ml (6 fl oz) chicken stock*
- *½–¾ tsp ground nutmeg*
- *salt and freshly cracked pepper*
- *grated Parmesan or romano cheese, to serve*

PASTA DOUGH

- *500 g (17½ oz) quinoa flour*
- *½ tsp salt*
- *5 extra large eggs*
- *1 tbsp olive oil*

For the pasta dough, place all the pasta ingredients in a food processor, process until ingredients come together into a ball. This takes time but the pasta will come together. No need to rest dough in the fidge before shaping. Use a pasta machine to roll the dough out into fettuccini or your favorite pasta shape.

Heat oil in a large, deep frying pan and brown chicken all over. Set chicken aside.

Add the scallions and garlic to the pan and cook for about a minute. Stir in the mushrooms and cook until soft, about 5 minutes. Add the cream, stock and nutmeg, stir well, bring to the boil then return the chicken to the pan and season. Cook, covered, on medium heat for 8–10 minutes until chicken is cooked and the sauce has thickened.

Cook the pasta in boiling salted water; fresh quinoa pasta only takes about 3–5 minutes to cook once the water comes back to the boil. Drain and throw the pasta into the pan with the chicken. Toss well, sprinkle with some grated parmesan or romano cheese and serve.

CHICKEN AND PRESERVED LEMON TAGINE WITH COCONUT QUINOA

Serves 4

Ingredients

- *1 kg (2 lb 3 oz) chicken thigh fillets*
- *1½ tsp ground cilantro (coriander)*
- *1 tsp ground turmeric*
- *1 tsp ground ginger*
- *1 tsp ground cumin*
- *salt and freshly ground black pepper*
- *1 large onion, halved and thinly sliced*
- *1 preserved lemon*
- *4 cloves garlic, chopped*
- *90 g (3½ oz) stuffed green olives*
- *a generous pinch of saffron*
- *olive oil*
- *120 ml (4 fl oz) water*

COCONUT QUINOA

- *275 g (10 oz) quinoa grain, rinsed and drained*
- *350 ml (12 fl oz) coconut milk*
- *350 ml (12 fl oz) hot water*
- *lemon zest*
- *cilantro (coriander), chopped*

Cut the chicken thigh fillets in half and place in a large plastic bag. Mix the cilantro, turmeric, ginger, cumin, salt and pepper together and sprinkle over chicken, give the bag a shake to coat the chicken.

Place half the onion slices in the bottom of a large frying pan which has a tight fitting lid, place the chicken pieces on top in a single layer and then cover with the remaining onion slices.

Remove and discard the pulp from the preserved lemon, chop the rind into small pieces and then scatter them over chicken, along with the garlic and olives. Sprinkle with saffron and a good drizzle of olive oil. Add the water, swirl the pan and cover tightly with lid. Bring to the boil, then reduce heat and simmer on low heat for 45–50 minutes, until the chicken is cooked and the onions are soft. Serve with coconut quinoa.

For the coconut quinoa: place the quinoa in a medium-sized saucepan with the coconut milk and water. Bring to the boil, cover and simmer on low heat for 10–15 minutes, until all the liquid has been absorbed. Lightly stir in the lemon zest and cilantro with a fork before serving with the chicken.

CHICKEN AND VEGETABLE LOAF

Serves 4-6

This chicken loaf is great for picnics—it is as delicious served cold as it is served warm.

Ingredients

- *500 g (17½ oz) ground/minced chicken*
- *1 large red onion, finely chopped*
- *2 cloves garlic, finely chopped*
- *2 tbsps finely chopped parsley*
- *2 tbsps fresh thyme leaves*
- *2 heaped tbsps horseradish (from a jar)*
- *½–1 red bell pepper (capsicum)*
- *150 g (5 oz) frozen peas, thawed*
- *80 g (3 oz) quinoa flakes*
- *1 tbsp olive oil*
- *2 eggs*
- *Salt and freshly cracked pepper*

Method

Preheat the oven to 200°C (400°F) and lightly oil a 25 cm (10 in) non-stick loaf tin.

Place the ground chicken in a large bowl and add the onion, garlic, parsley, thyme and horseradish, and mix.

Cut the bell pepper in half, remove the seeds and membrane, and cut into very small pieces.

Drain the peas of any water after thawing and add pepper and peas to the mince. Stir the quinoa flakes, oil and eggs and season with salt and pepper into the chicken mixture. Mix well to thoroughly combine.

Place mince mixture into the prepared loaf tin and bake for 45–50 minutes until golden brown on top.

Remove from the oven, cover with foil and rest for 5–10 minutes before turning out on to a serving platter.

Slice and serve with your favorite chutney or sauce.

CHICKEN WITH BACON, SAGE AND ONION STUFFING

Serves 4

Ingredients

- *1–2 tbsps extra virgin olive oil*
- *1 large onion, finely chopped*
- *2–3 rashers bacon, rind removed and chopped*
- *2 cloves garlic, finely chopped*
- *80 g (3 oz) quinoa flakes*
- *2 tbsps chopped sage leaves*
- *1½ tbsps chopped chives*
- *2 tbsps chopped fresh flat-leaf parsley*
- *zest of 1 lemon*
- *Salt and freshly cracked black pepper*
- *1 extra large egg*
- *1 whole chicken (about 1.8 kg/4 lb)*
- *lemon juice*
- *sweet paprika*

Method

Preheat the oven to 190°C (375°F).

Heat the oil in a large frying pan and sauté onion and bacon until soft and golden, stir in the garlic and take off the heat. Cool slightly.

Place the bacon, onion and garlic into a bowl with the quinoa flakes, sage, chives, parsley and lemon zest. Season with salt and pepper. Add the egg then mix together to thoroughly combine. Mixture should be moist and hold together.

Remove any excess fat from the chicken, rinse and pat dry with kitchen paper. Place the stuffing mixture into the cavity of the chicken and secure the opening with a small metal skewer.

Place the chicken into a baking dish and drizzle with some extra virgin olive oil and a good squeeze of lemon juice. Season the chicken with a little salt and pepper and sprinkle with ground paprika.

Bake for 1 hour 10 minutes to 1 hour and 20 minutes, until the chicken is cooked and a deep golden brown. Baste chicken every now and then with pan juices.

Chicken is cooked when tested with a metal skewer in the thick thigh area and the juices run clear. Cover with foil and allow to rest for 10–15 minutes before serving.

BAKED 'FRIED' CHICKEN

Serves 3–6

Chicken thigh cutlets are also known as chicken chops and are the thigh with just one main thick bone left in them. They are great for use in dishes such as this one or in casseroles and curries as the thigh meat can take longer cooking times and the bone adds more flavor. You can use breast meat, drumsticks, whole chicken legs with a portion of the backbone attached, or wings if you prefer instead. I sometimes use a whole chicken, which I segment into pieces.

Ingredients

- *6 chicken thigh cutlets/chops, with skin on*
- *240 ml (8 fl oz) buttermilk*
- *salt and freshly ground black pepper*
- *lemon juice, for serving*

COATING

- *125 g (4½ oz) quinoa flour*
- *1 tsp smoked paprika*
- *1 tsp sweet paprika*
- *1 tsp celery salt*
- *1 tsp ground turmeric*
- *½ tsp chili powder*
- *finely grated zest of 1 lemon*
- *drizzle of olive oil*

Method

Buy even-sized chicken pieces. Make three incisions along each cutlet, cutting through the skin and a bit of the meat part.

Place into a bowl with the buttermilk and a little salt and pepper. Coat well, making sure you rub the buttermilk into each incision and the chicken is completely covered with it.

Leave to marinade in the fridge for at least 2–4 hours. The longer the better, even overnight is fine.

Preheat oven to 200°C (400°F) and line a baking tray with non-stick baking paper.

Make the coating by mixing the quinoa flour with the smoked and sweet paprika, celery salt, turmeric, chili and lemon zest. Make sure all the spices are evenly distributed through the flour.

Give the chicken a little shake to remove any excess buttermilk, as you don't want it dripping in liquid, then coat completely with the coating mixture.

Place chicken on the baking tray and drizzle very lightly with a little olive oil, place in the oven and bake for 40–50 minutes until the chicken is cooked and golden brown.

Rest for 5 minutes loosely covered in foil, before serving with a squeeze of lemon juice. Delicious!

CHICKEN BREASTS WITH CRANBERRIES, ORANGE AND PISTACHIO

Serves 4

This stuffing mixture is really lovely to use and is ideal as a stuffing for the Christmas turkey.

Ingredients

- *1 tbsp olive oil*
- *1 red onion, finely chopped*
- *2–3 cloves garlic, finely chopped*
- *120 g (4½ oz) quinoa flakes*
- *1 tbsp chopped chives*
- *1 tbsp chopped thyme*
- *60 g (2 oz) shelled pistachio nuts, chopped*
- *60 g (2 oz) dried cranberries*
- *Juice and rind of 1 orange*
- *Salt and freshly cracked black pepper*
- *1 extra large egg*
- *4 chicken breast fillets, with skin on*
- *Lemon juice*
- *Olive oil, extra*
- *Sweet paprika*

Preheat oven to 180°C (350°F) and line a baking tray with non-stick baking parchment/paper.

Heat the oil in a frying pan and sauté the onion until soft, stir in garlic and cook for about 1 minute. Remove from the heat.

Place the quinoa flakes into a bowl with the chives, thyme and pistachio nuts and cranberries.

Stir the orange juice and rind into the onion and garlic mixture, and season with salt and pepper. Add the egg and mix thoroughly.

With your fingers, gently separate some of the skin from the fillet to make a pocket.

Divide stuffing mixture equally between fillets and spread into each pocket. Ensure the filling is completely covered by the skin.

Place the chicken breasts on the baking tray, skin side up. Squeeze lemon juice on top, drizzle with a little extra olive oil, season with salt and pepper and sprinkle with a little paprika.

Bake for 20–30 minutes until chicken is cooked and skin golden. Remove from the oven and cover with foil to rest for about 10 minutes before serving.

HONEY AND SESAME LEMON CHICKEN

Serves 4

Ingredients

- *90 g (3½ oz) quinoa flour*
- *1 tsp Chinese five spice powder*
- *1 tsp cracked black pepper*
- *salt, to taste*
- *1 egg*
- *240 ml (8 fl oz) soda water*
- *340 g (12 oz) honey*
- *juice of 1 lemon*
- *1 tbsp sesame seeds*
- *oil, for frying*
- *1 kg (2 lb 4 oz) chicken breast tenderloins*
- *60 g (2½ oz) quinoa flour, extra*

Combine the flour, five spice powder, pepper and salt together.

Make a well in the centre, add the egg and slowly whisk in with the soda water and mix until you have a smooth batter mixture.

Place the honey, lemon juice and sesame seeds into a small saucepan and gently heat through until it comes to the boil. Continue to simmer on low heat for a few minutes until the sesame seeds just start to change color. Remove from heat.

Meanwhile, start to heat the oil in a deep frying pan with enough oil to just come up half way the depth of the tenderloins.

Dredge the tenderloins in the extra flour then dip into the batter, making sure the chicken is completely covered. When the oil is hot, cook the tenderloins until golden on both sides.

Remove from the pan with a slotted spoon and drain on kitchen paper, keep warm until all the chicken is cooked.

When all the chicken is cooked place on a serving platter and drizzle the warmed honey sauce all over. Serve immediately.

CHICKEN FILLETS WITH PANCETTA, OLIVES AND SUN-DRIED TOMATOES

Serves 4

This is a great dinner-party dish, especially if you or any of your guests are wheat- or gluten-intolerant and you want to make something special which can be enjoyed by everyone.

Ingredients

- *4 chicken breast fillets*
- *40 g (1½ oz) quinoa flakes*
- *4 slices pancetta, chopped*
- *8 kalamata olives, chopped*
- *90 g (3 oz) sun- or semi-dried tomatoes, chopped*
- *1 tbsp grated parmesan cheese (optional)*
- *1 tsp dried oregano leaves*
- *1 sallion (spring onion), finely sliced*
- *1 tbsp extra virgin olive oil*
- *1 tsp balsamic vinegar*
- *2 tbsp water*
- *salt and freshly ground black pepper*
- *parsley, chopped, for garnish*

SAUCE

- *400 g (14 oz) can diced tomatoes*
- *60 ml (2 fl oz) water*
- *1 tsp dried oregano leaves*
- *salt and pepper*

Preheat the oven to 175°C (340°F).

Cut a deep pocket into the chicken fillets, taking care not to cut right through.

Combine the quinoa flakes with the pancetta, olives, tomatoes, cheese, oregano, scallions, olive oil, vinegar and water. Add salt and pepper to taste, but season carefully as the pancetta and olives and parmesan can be quite salty.

Spoon the filling into the pockets in the chicken and smooth the top part of the fillet over the filling to enclose.

Mix all the sauce ingredients together and pour into a baking dish. Place the fillets on top, drizzle with extra virgin olive oil and bake for 25–30 minutes, until the chicken is cooked. Add a little extra water to the sauce if necessary during cooking.

Serve with the sauce spooned over the chicken and garnished with parsley.

ROAST CHICKEN WITH BACON, MUSTARD AND HERB STUFFING

Serves 4–6

Ingredients

- *1 chicken, about 2 kg (4 lb 8 oz)*
- *1 tbsp olive oil*
- *juice of 1 lemon*
- *1 tsp dried oregano leaves*
- *salt and pepper*

STUFFING

- *1 tbsp olive oil*
- *1small onion, finely chopped*
- *3 bacon rashers, rind removed, chopped*
- *60 g (2½ oz) quinoa flakes*
- *1 tbsp prepared English mustard*
- *2 tbsp chopped flatleaf parsley*
- *2 tbsp chopped chives*
- *1 tsp fresh thyme leaves*
- *1 tsp dried oregano leaves*
- *zest of 1 lemon*
- *1 egg*
- *freshly ground black pepper*

Preheat the oven to 170°C (340°F).

To prepare the stuffing, heat the oil in a small frying pan and brown the onion and bacon. Turn into a bowl and add all the other stuffing ingredients. Mix well until thoroughly combined.

Remove any excess fat from the chicken, rinse under cold water and thoroughly pat dry with kitchen paper. Place in a roasting dish. Spoon the stuffing mixture into the chicken cavity and secure the opening with a metal skewer. Rub the skin with olive oil, pour over the lemon juice, sprinkle with oregano and season with salt and pepper. Roast for about 1½–1¾ hours, until the chicken is cooked and golden.

You can add your favorite vegetables to the roasting dish around the chicken if you wish. Cover the chicken with foil if it starts to brown too quickly.

SPICY CHICKEN WITH HERBED QUINOA

Serves 4

Ingredients

- 4 chicken breast fillets
- 2 tsps ground cumin
- 2 tsps ground cilantro (coriander)
- 1 tsp ground turmeric
- 2–3 cloves garlic, finely grated
- 1 tbsp extra virgin olive oil
- juice and zest of 1 lemon
- salt and freshly cracked pepper
- 275 g (10 oz) quinoa, rinsed and drained
- 700 ml (24 fl oz) water
- 2 Lebanese cucumbers, cubed
- 1 red onion, finely chopped
- 4 scallions (spring onions), sliced
- 20 g (¾ oz) chopped cilantro (coriander)
- 20 g (¾ oz) chopped mint
- 20 g (¾ oz) chopped flat-leaf parsley
- juice of 1–1½ lemons, extra
- 3–4 tbsps extra virgin
- olive oil
- salt and freshly cracked pepper
- extra cilantro (coriander) leaves, to garnish

Combine the chicken, cumin, ground cilantro, turmeric, garlic, olive oil, lemon juice and zest, season with salt and pepper, and leave to marinate for at least 30 minutes.

Place the quinoa into a medium saucepan with the water. Bring to the boil, reduce the heat and simmer, covered, for about 10 minutes until all the water is absorbed. Remove from the heat and leave to stand, covered, until you need it.

Cook the chicken by grilling, lightly pan-frying or baking in the oven. Once it is cooked, cover with foil and rest for about 10 minutes before serving.

While the chicken is cooking, mix together the quinoa, cucumber, onion, scallions, cilantro leaves, mint and parsley.

Whisk together the lemon juice, olive oil and salt and pepper, and toss through the quinoa.

Slice the chicken and serve with the herbed quinoa. Garnish with extra cilantro leaves and wedges of lemon.

CHILI AND GARLIC CHICKEN

Serves 6.

Use as many or as few chilies as you like and either leave the seeds in or remove them or do half with seeds in half without—it is entirely up to your own personal taste.

Ingredients

- *275 g (10 oz) quinoa, rinsed and drained*
- *700 ml (24 fl oz) chicken stock or water*
- *1 kg (2 lb 4 oz) chicken thigh fillets, trimmed and cut into thickish slices*
- *1 tbsp paprika*
- *1 tbsp extra virgin olive oil*
- *Salt*
- *2–3 tbsps extra virgin olive oil, extra*
- *4–5 large cloves garlic, finely chopped*
- *8 scallions (spring onions), sliced diagonally into large pieces*
- *6–8 long red chilies, sliced*
- *150 g (5 oz) sugar snap peas, string removed*
- *175 ml (6 fl oz) white wine*
- *zest and juice of 1–2 limes*
- *salt, extra*

Method

Place the quinoa in a saucepan with the stock or water. Bring to the boil, reduce the heat, cover and simmer for 10–12 minutes until all the water is absorbed. Remove from the heat and leave to stand, covered, while you prepare the chicken.

Coat the chicken with the paprika and 1 tbsp of oil and season with a little salt.

Heat the extra oil in a large, deep-frying pan and, when the oil is hot, cook the chicken until golden and cooked through on both sides. Remove from the pan and keep warm.

In the same pan, add a little extra oil if needed and sauté the garlic, scallions, chilies and sugar snap peas for 2–3 minutes on medium-high heat stirring constantly until they soften and take on some color.

Pour in the wine and deglaze the pan, cook for about 1 minute until the alcohol evaporates, then stir in as much zest and lime juice as you like and season with salt to taste.

Add the quinoa and chicken to the pan and gently toss everything together. Cook on low heat for 1–2 minutes until heated through. Serve with wedges of lime.

TANDOORI CHICKEN

Serves 4

Ingredients

- *1 kg (2 lb 4 oz) chicken thigh fillets*
- *1 tbsp Greek or natural yogurt*
- *3 tbsp tandoori paste*
- *3 tbsp extra virgin olive oil*
- *1 large brown onion, chopped*
- *3 cloves garlic, finely chopped*
- *275 g (10 oz) quinoa, rinsed and drained*
- *700 ml (24 fl oz) hot chicken stock or water*
- *salt and freshly ground black pepper*
- *250 g (9 oz) green beans, cut into large pieces*
- *handful of cilantro (coriander), roughly chopped*
- *lime juice, for serving*
- *red chili, sliced, for garnish*
- *Greek (natural) yogurt, for serving*

Method

Cut chicken into strips. Mix with the yogurt and tandoori paste and leave to marinade for at least half an hour, longer if possible.

Heat oil in a large, deep frying pan and brown chicken on high heat until it takes on some color, about 8 minutes. Remove from heat.

Add onion to the pan and cook for 3–4 minutes until soft (you may need to add a little more oil to the pan). Stir in the garlic and cook for 30 seconds.

Add quinoa, stir well, return chicken to the pan then pour in stock or water and season with salt and pepper to taste.

Bring to the boil, reduce the heat, cover and simmer for 15 minutes. Stir in the beans and simmer for another 5 minutes.

Stir in cilantro and serve with a good squeeze of lime juice, slices of red chili and Greek yogurt.

SPANISH CHICKEN

Serves 4

This is one of those quick and really easy-to-prepare meals that are perfect for dinner after work or for when unexpected guests drop by.

Ingredients

- *1 kg (2 lb 4 oz) chicken thigh fillets, skin removed*
- *½–1 tsp smoked paprika*
- *1 tbsp extra virgin olive oil*
- *1 tbsp ghee*
- *1 large onion, chopped*
- *3 cloves garlic, finely chopped*
- *½ tsp saffron strands*
- *zest of 1 lemon*
- *275 g (10 oz) quinoa, rinsed and drained*
- *salt and pepper*
- *700 ml (24 fl oz) hot chicken stock*
- *180 g (6 oz) stuffed green olives*
- *20 g (¾ oz) chopped flat-leaf parsley*
- *lemon juice*

Method

Rub the chicken with the paprika until well coated. Heat the oil and melt ghee in a large, deep frying pan and brown the chicken all over on medium-high heat until almost half-cooked and a deep golden color. Remove from the pan and keep warm by covering with foil.

Add the onion to the pan and cook until soft. Stir in the garlic and cook until fragrant.

Lightly crush the saffron and add to the pan with the lemon zest, and season with salt and pepper.

Add the quinoa and stock, stirring everything together well, then return the chicken pieces to the pan and nestle in with the quinoa.

Bring to the boil, reduce the heat, cover and simmer for about 10 minutes. Scatter the olives over the chicken, cover and simmer for another 5–8 minutes until all the liquid is absorbed. Take off the heat and leave to stand for 5–10 minutes.

Sprinkle with the parsley and lemon juice and serve.

SPICY DUCK WITH GINGER AND CHILI QUINOA

Serves 4

Ingredients

- *1 clove garlic*
- *1 tsp ground ginger*
- *½–1 tsp chili flakes*
- *1 tbsp tamari soy sauce*
- *1 tbsp honey*
- *2 tsp olive oil*
- *juice and zest of 1 lime*
- *½ tsp five spice powder*
- *salt, to taste*
- *4 duck breasts, with the skins*
- *lime, for serving*

GINGER AND CHILI QUINOA

- *2 tbsp olive oil*
- *2 cloves garlic, grated*
- *1–2 long red chilies, sliced or*
- *de-seeded and chopped*
- *1 knob of ginger, peeled and thinly sliced*
- *16 scallions (spring onions), sliced diagonally*
- *½ tsp ground turmeric*
- *275 g (10 oz) quinoa, rinsed and drained*
- *2 star anise*
- *700 ml (24 fl oz) hot chicken stock*
- *salt, to taste*
- *extra scallions (spring onions) and chilies, sliced, for garnish*

Method

Make a marinade by mixing together the garlic, ginger, chili, tamari, honey, oil, lime juice and zest, five spice powder and salt. Make 2–3 cuts across the skin of each duck breast, and rub all over with the marinade; make sure you get right into the cuts. Marinade for at least half an hour.

Heat a large frying pan until hot, place the duck into the pan, skin side down, cook until browned and the fat has rendered out. Keep turning the duck and cook for about 15 minutes for medium done. Remove from the heat and cover with foil to rest. Or, after browning, you can finish cooking the duck in the oven.

In the meantime, make the quinoa by heating the oil in a large frying pan. Add the garlic, chilies and ginger and sauté 1–2 minutes until soft. Stir in the scallions and turmeric. Mix in the quinoa and star anise, pour in the stock and season. Bring to the boil, reduce the heat, cover and simmer for 12–15 minutes until all stock is absorbed. Garnish with extra chilies and scallions and serve with the duck and lime juice.

PARMESAN AND HERB-CRUSTED CHICKEN SCHNITZEL

Serves 4

Ingredients

- 4 halves chicken breast fillets
- 120 g (4½ oz) quinoa flakes
- 120 g (4½ oz) parmesan, grated
- 2 tbsp basil, finely chopped
- 2 tbsp chives, finely chopped
- 2 tbsp parsley, finely chopped
- grated rind of 1 lemon
- salt and freshly cracked black pepper
- 60 g (2½ oz) quinoa flour
- 2 eggs, lightly beaten
- olive oil, for frying
- lemon juice, for serving

Place the chicken breast half between two sheets of plastic wrap and gently pound with a meat mallet or rolling pin until about 5 mm (¼ in) thick. If the pieces of chicken are too big then cut each one in half.

Combine quinoa flakes with the cheese, herbs, lemon rind, salt and pepper.

Dust each piece of chicken with flour then dip into the beaten egg. Gently press into the flake mixture to coat well.

Heat some olive oil in a large frying pan and shallow-fry the chicken pieces in batches until golden and cooked. Drain on kitchen paper.

Serve with a good squeeze of lemon juice and a lovely salad.

Seafood

LEMON AND CHIVE–CRUMBED FISH FILLETS WITH TOSSED QUINOA SALAD

Serves 4–6

I find fish cooked this way is always a great hit and a good way to get kids to eat fish. As much as I love fish and chips, you really can't beat this healthier version.

Ingredients

- *200 g (7 oz) quinoa flakes*
- *zest of 1 large lemon*
- *3 tbsps chopped chives*
- *½–1 tsp chili flakes (optional)*
- *Salt and freshly cracked black pepper*
- *125 g (4½ oz) quinoa flour*
- *1 kg (2 lb 4 oz) boneless fish fillets*
- *2–3 extra large eggs, lightly beaten*
- *oil, for shallow-frying*
- *pepper*
- *lemon juice, to serve*

SALAD

- *125 g (4½ oz) quinoa, rinsed and drained*
- *315 ml (10½ fl oz) water*
- *green salad leaves*
- *1 cucumber, halved and sliced*
- *1–2 tomatoes, cut into thin wedges*
- *1 small red onion, halved then thinly sliced*
- *extra virgin olive oil*
- *lemon juice*
- *salt and freshly cracked black pepper*

Method

Combine the quinoa flakes with the lemon zest, chives, chili flakes (if using), and salt and pepper.

Place the quinoa flour into a bowl. Dust the fish fillets with the quinoa flour then dip into the beaten egg.

Press the fish into the quinoa flake mixture and coat well.

Heat the oil in a large frying pan until hot, and gently shallow-fry the fillets on a medium-high heat for about 3–5 minutes each side, depending on the thickness of the fish. Remove from the pan and drain on kitchen paper, then serve hot with a good squeeze of lemon juice and the Tossed Quinoa Salad.

Place the quinoa in a small saucepan with the water. Bring to the boil, reduce the heat, cover and simmer for 10 minutes until all the water is absorbed. Take off the heat and leave to stand, covered, for 10 minutes before cooling completely.

To finish off the salad, toss together the cooled, cooked quinoa with the other salad ingredients.

SPANISH-STYLE MUSSELS

Serves 4

Ingredients

- *3 tbsp extra virgin olive oil*
- *1 medium red onion, finely chopped*
- *6 scallions (spring onions), sliced*
- *1 green pepper (capsicum), seeded and sliced*
- *1 red pepper (capsicum), seeded and sliced*
- *4–5 cloves garlic, finely chopped*
- *120 ml (4 fl oz) white wine*
- *a good pinch of saffron threads*
- *2 x 400 g (14 oz) cans diced tomatoes*
- *½–1 tsp dried chili flakes*
- *1 kg (2.2 lb) mussels*
- *185 g (6 oz) quinoa grain, rinsed and drained*
- *175 ml (6 fl oz) hot water*
- *salt and pepper*
- *180 g (6 oz) green stuffed olives*
- *a handful chopped flatleaf parsley*
- *lemon wedges for serving*

Heat the olive oil in a large frying pan and sauté the onion, shallots and peppers until soft, then stir in the garlic and cook for 30 seconds. Pour in the wine, deglaze the pan and cook for 1–2 minutes. Add the saffron, tomatoes and chili, stir and cook on low heat, covered, for about 5–7 minutes until the sauce thickens.

Meanwhile, prepare the mussels by pulling out the beards and scraping off any barnacles; rinse well. Discard any that are open.

Add the quinoa to the pan with the water, season with salt and pepper, stir, and simmer, covered, for about 7 minutes, stirring occasionally. Watch it to make sure it does not dry out—avoid adding any more liquid because the mussels will release a lot of their own liquor. Add the mussels, cover and cook for another 8–10 minutes, stirring occasionally until the quinoa is cooked and the mussels are open.

Stir in the olives and parsley and serve with lemon wedges.

FRIED 'RICE'

Serves 6

This is a family favorite in our house; it is just so much lighter to digest than the usual fried rice.

Ingredients

- *275 g (10 oz) quinoa, rinsed and drained*
- *700 ml (24 fl oz) water*
- *1 tbsp oil*
- *2 eggs*
- *1 tsp soy sauce*
- *1 tbsp water*
- *2 tbsp oil extra*
- *½ tsp sesame oil*
- *3 rashers bacon, rind removed and diced*
- *500 g (17½ oz) green shrimp (prawns), peeled and de-veined*
- *8 scallions (spring onions), sliced*
- *75 g (3 oz) frozen peas*
- *200 g (7 oz) fresh baby corn spears or*
- *1 x 400 g (14 oz) canned, drained*
- *2–3 tbsp light tamari soy sauce*
- *soy sauce, for serving*
- *scallions (spring onions), chopped, for serving*

Method

Place quinoa in a small saucepan with the water, bring to the boil, then reduce the heat, cover and simmer for 10 minutes until all the water is absorbed. Remove from heat and spread out onto a tray to cool and dry out completely.

Lightly whisk the eggs with the soy sauce and water. Heat the oil in a wok until hot, add the beaten eggs and swirl around to form an omelette.

When the eggs have set, tilt wok away from you and, using a spatula, carefully roll up the omelette. Remove from the wok and slice into thin strips and set aside.

Heat extra oil and sesame oil in the wok, add the bacon, shrimp and scallions including as much of the green part as is usable. Cook on high heat, stirring constantly, until the shrimp change color and the bacon starts to crisp up.

Add the peas and corn spears and continue stirring for 2–3 minutes.

Stir in the soy sauce and the cooled quinoa and continue cooking for 3–4 minutes until quinoa is heated through. Gently stir in the egg strips and serve with an extra drizzle of soy sauce and chopped scallions.

THAI FISH CAKES

Makes about 20

I find that coating the fish cakes with the quinoa flakes gives an added crunch and helps them remain moist and not go rubbery.

Ingredients

- *80 g (3 oz) quinoa flakes*
- *2 tbsps finely chopped cilantro (coriander) leaves*
- *1 small red onion, chopped*
- *4 cloves garlic, chopped*
- *1–2 red chilies*
- *1 knob about 2.5 cm (1 in) galangal or ginger, sliced*
- *1 stalk lemongrass, sliced*
- *1 kaffir lime leaf, thinly sliced*
- *500 g (17½ oz) white fish fillets*
- *1 extra large egg*
- *3 tbsps chopped cilantro (coriander) roots and leaves*
- *½ tsp ground cumin powder*
- *2–3 tbsps fish sauce*
- *90 g (3 oz) fresh green beans, very thinly sliced*
- *oil for frying*
- *lime juice, for serving*
- *sweet chili sauce, for serving*

Mix the quinoa flakes and cilantro together and set aside.

Place the onion, garlic, chilies, galangal, lemongrass and kaffir lime leaf into a food processor and process until the ingredients are finely minced.

Remove any bones from the fish, cut into chunks and add to the processor with the egg, cilantro, cumin and fish sauce and continue processing until you get a well combined mixture that still has some texture to it. Place the mixture into a bowl and mix in the beans. Roll out spoonfuls of mixture into a ball and flatten slightly then press into the flake and cilantro mixture.

Heat some oil until hot and shallow-fry the fish cakes until golden on both sides, about 2 minutes each side. Take care not to overcook them.

Remove with a slotted spoon and place on kitchen paper. Serve immediately with fresh lime juice and/or sweet chili sauce.

SEAFOOD PAELLA

Serves 6–8

Traditionally, a proper paella is supposed to have a slightly burnt and crunchy crust at the bottom of the pan which everyone fights over as it is considered to be the best part. The amount of cooking time above is usually sufficient to cook the seafood and quinoa completely but to also allow for a crunchy base to develop. You can use whatever combination of seafood you prefer. You will need a pan or paella pan that has a large cooking surface to get the best results when cooking this dish but to also accommodate all the seafood and other ingredients.

Ingredients

- *4 tbsp extra virgin olive oil*
- *1 large onion, finely chopped*
- *1 large red pepper (capsicum), seeded and chopped*
- *4 cloves garlic, finely chopped*
- *370 g (12½ oz) quinoa, rinsed and drained*
- *1 x 400 g (14 oz) tin diced tomatoes*
- *500 g (17½ oz) calamari tubes, sliced*
- *830 ml (28 fl oz) fish or chicken stock*
- *1 tsp saffron strands*
- *sea salt and ground black pepper*
- *750 g (1 lb 10 oz) large green shrimp (prawns), unpeeled*
- *750 g (1 lb 10 oz) mussels, scrubbed*
- *150 g (5 oz) frozen peas*
- *flat-leaf parsley, chopped*
- *lemon wedges, for garnish*

Heat olive oil in a large, deep frying pan or a paella dish if you have one and sauté onion and pepper until onion is soft and golden.

Stir in garlic and quinoa then pour in tomatoes, sliced calamari, stock and saffron, season with salt and pepper, cover loosely with lid or foil and cook for about 12 minutes.

Arrange shrimp and mussels on top then cover again and cook for another 10 minutes, adding more stock if necessary but only if the pan is completely dry.

Gently stir in the peas and cook, covered, for another 5–10 minutes until quinoa is cooked.

Sprinkle with parsley and a good squeeze of lemon juice. Serve with lemon wedges arranged on top.

RAINBOW TROUT WITH ALMONDS AND TARRAGON

Serves 2

Ingredients

- *45 g (1½ oz) flaked almonds*
- *1 large tomato*
- *45 g (1½ oz) butter*
- *4 scallions (spring onions), finely chopped*
- *50 g (2 oz) quinoa flakes*
- *2 cloves garlic, finely chopped*
- *1 tbsp tarragon, chopped*
- *1 tbsp baby capers, drained*
- *juice of ½ a lemon*
- *salt and freshly cracked pepper*
- *2 rainbow trout, scaled and gutted, about 350 g (12 oz) each*
- *extra virgin olive oil, for drizzling*
- *lemon juice, for drizzling*
- *salt and freshly cracked black pepper*
- *tarragon sprigs, for garnish*
- *lemon wedges, for garnish*

Place almonds in a non-stick frying pan and toast until golden. There is no need to add any oil or butter to the pan but keep an eye on them and toss regularly. Remove from heat and transfer onto a plate.

Preheat the oven to 190°C (375°F) and line a baking tray with non-stick baking parchment/paper.

Skin the tomato by cutting a small cross at the bottom and then plunging the tomato into boiling water for about 30 seconds then remove. Skin should peel off quite easily. Chop the tomato finely and set aside.

Melt the butter in a medium-sized frying pan, add the scallions and cook on medium-high heat for 1–2 minutes until they start to change color. Stir in the quinoa flakes and garlic and cook 2–3 minutes, tossing regularly to coat the flakes in the butter and scallions. Mix in the tomato, tarragon, capers, some lemon juice and two-thirds of the almonds. Season well with salt and pepper and cool slightly.

Season inside of each fish and fill each one with stuffing mixture, secure the opening with metal skewers. Place the fish on the baking tray, drizzle with some extra virgin olive oil, lemon juice and season with salt and pepper. Bake for 20–30 minutes until the trout is cooked. Serve garnished with a scattering of the remaining almonds, some sprigs of tarragon and lemon wedges.

SHRIMP CUTLETS

Serves 4

To butterfly shrimp first peel them. After peeling the shrimp make a cut deep into the back of each one without cutting right through, remove the vein then gently flatten the shrimp. What you should be left with is a shrimp that has been almost sliced in half and opened like a book with the tail intact.

I have allowed six shrimp per person and I like to use quite large shrimp as they tend to shrink during cooking. You might like to vary the amount according to your diners' appetites.

Ingredients

- *24 extra large green shrimp (prawns)*
- *120 g (4½ oz) quinoa flakes*
- *1 tsp ground paprika*
- *zest of 1 lemon*
- *salt and freshly cracked pepper*
- *olive oil, for frying*
- *lemon juice, for serving*

Peel and de-vein shrimp leaving tail intact and butterfly them (see method above).

Mix together the quinoa flakes, paprika, lemon zest, salt and pepper.

Coat the shrimp in the flake mixture, pressing down to make sure they are well coated and the coating sticks to the shrimp.

Heat enough oil on medium heat in a large frying pan until hot. There should be enough oil to just come up about halfway up the shrimp.

Add the shrimp and shallow-fry until golden on both sides and the shrimp are cooked.

Sprinkle with lemon juice and serve.

MUSTARD-CRUSTED SALMON WITH DILL AND LEMON

Serves 4

A delicious and different way to serve salmon. It is lovely for a luncheon served with a big salad.

Ingredients

- *4 salmon fillets, about 200 g (7 oz) each*
- *2 tbsp Dijon mustard*
- *3 tbsp chopped dill*
- *2 tbsp chopped flatleaf parsley*
- *1 large clove garlic, grated*
- *zest of 1 lemon*
- *2–3 tbsp lemon juice*
- *1 scallion (spring onion), finely sliced including the greens*
- *1 tbsp olive oil*
- *80 g (3 oz) quinoa flakes*
- *salt and freshly ground black pepper*
- *lemon juice to serve*
- *sprigs of dill to serve*

Preheat the oven to 180°C (350°F).

Trim the salmon fillets to an even shape and place, skin side down, on a roasting tray that has been lined with baking paper.

Place the mustard in a bowl with the dill, parsley, garlic, lemon zest, juice, scallion and olive oil. Mix thoroughly to combine. Mix in the quinoa flakes, salt and pepper. Use your hands to mix and squeeze the mixture together so it holds.

Divide the mixture into four and spread evenly on top of each fillet. Drizzle with extra virgin olive oil and roast for 15–20 minutes until the topping is golden and the salmon is cooked.

Serve with a squeeze of lemon juice and sprigs of dill.

CURRIED SHRIMP WITH TOASTED COCONUT QUINOA

Serves 4

Ingredients

- *2 tbsp olive oil*
- *2 medium onions, halved then sliced*
- *3 cloves garlic, finely chopped*
- *2 tbsp curry powder*
- *1 tsp ground cumin*
- *2 tbsp tamari soy sauce*
- *2–3 medium carrots, sliced*
- *salt and freshly cracked pepper*
- *350 ml (12 fl oz) water or fish stock*
- *1 kg (2 lb 4 oz) peeled green shrimp (prawns)*
- *225 g (8 oz) frozen peas*
- *lemon juice, for serving*

TOASTED COCONUT QUINOA

- *370 g (12½ oz) quinoa, rinsed and drained*
- *590 ml (20 fl oz) water*
- *1 x 400 g (14 oz) can coconut milk*
- *75 g (3 oz) coconut flakes, shredded*

Heat oil in a large saucepan and sauté onion on medium heat until soft and lightly browned. Add the garlic and cook for about 1 minute.

Stir in the curry powder and cumin and cook for another minute, then add the soy sauce and carrots. Season with salt and pepper then pour in the water or stock. Stir the pan, making sure to scrap the bottom of the pan, to release all the flavors that have developed.

Bring to the boil then reduce the heat, cover and simmer for about 10 minutes.

Add the shrimp, bring back to the boil then reduce the heat, cover and simmer on low heat for another 10 minutes or until the shrimp are cooked. Stir in the peas and simmer for 5 minutes more. Serve over a bed of toasted coconut quinoa with some lemon juice squeezed over.

To make the toasted coconut quinoa, place the quinoa in a medium saucepan with the water and coconut milk, bring to the boil, then reduce the heat, cover and simmer for 12–15 minutes until all the liquid is absorbed. Dry-roast the coconut flakes in a small, non-stick frying pan, turning and tossing regularly so it doesn't burn until it is a light golden color. Using a fork, toss the toasted coconut through the quinoa and serve with the curried shrimp.

MOROCCAN-STYLE BAKED FISH

Serves 4

You can also prepare a whole fish using this method, just use part of the mixture inside the fish and cover the outside with the remainder.

Ingredients

- *3 tbsp extra virgin olive oil*
- *6 scallions (spring onions), sliced*
- *3 cloves garlic, finely chopped*
- *½ tsp ground cilantro (coriander)*
- *1 tsp cilantro (coriander) seeds, left whole*
- *1 tsp ground cumin*
- *½ tsp cumin seeds, left whole*
- *1 tsp sweet paprika*
- *½ tsp chili flakes*
- *1 tsp ground ginger*
- *juice and zest of 1 lemon*
- *½ bunch flat-leaf parsley, very finely chopped*
- *½ bunch fresh cilantro (coriander), including roots and stems, very finely chopped*
- *²/ cup water*
- *80 g (3 oz) quinoa flakes*
- *salt and freshly ground black pepper*
- *extra virgin olive oil, extra*
- *lemon juice, extra*
- *4 largish snapper steaks*
- *extra virgin olive oil, for serving*
- *lemon juice, for serving*

Method

Preheat oven to 190°C (375°F).

Heat the oil in a medium-sized frying pan and sauté the scallions until they start to change color. Add the garlic and cook for about 30 seconds until fragrant. Stir in the ground cilantro and cilantro seeds, ground cumin and cumin seeds, paprika, chili and ginger and cook for about 1 minute. Add a little more oil if mixture is too dry and starting to burn.

Add the lemon juice, zest, parsley, fresh cilantro, water and quinoa flakes and season with salt and pepper. Stir and cook for about 1–2 minutes until the herbs collapse and the quinoa has mixed in with all the other flavors and the mixture resembles a moist paste. Remove from heat.

Place fish onto a greased, shallow baking dish and season with salt and pepper. Cover each piece of fish with evenly divided quinoa mixture and drizzle with extra virgin olive oil and a squeeze of lemon juice. Cover with foil and bake for about 15 minutes then remove the foil and bake for a further 10 minutes or so until fish is cooked. Drizzle with extra virgin olive oil and a good squeeze of lemon juice to serve.

SHRIMP 'RISOTTO'

Serves 4

You may hear and read that the Italians never ever sprinkle parmesan cheese on any seafood pasta or risotto dish. This is a very individual thing—in my family we always have, and my dear grandmother would be absolutely horrified if she thought we were doing it any differently.

Ingredients

- *3 tbsp olive oil*
- *1 onion, finely chopped*
- *3 scallions (spring onions), sliced*
- *2 large cloves garlic, finely chopped*
- *185 g (6 oz) quinoa grain, rinsed and drained*
- *120 ml (4 fl oz) white wine*
- *1 x 400 g (14 oz) can diced tomatoes*
- *salt and freshly ground black pepper*
- *480 ml (16 fl oz) hot water*
- *500 g (1 lb 2 oz) peeled and deveined shrimp (prawns)*
- *75 g (3 oz) frozen peas*
- *a knob of butter*
- *2 tbsp chopped flatleaf parsley*
- *grated parmesan (optional)*

Heat the olive oil in a large saucepan and cook the onions and scallions on medium heat for about 5 minutes until soft. Stir in the garlic. Add the quinoa to the pan and stir. Add the wine and cook until the alcohol has evaporated and all the liquid has been absorbed. Stir in the tomatoes, salt, pepper and hot water.

Cover and cook on a low simmer for 10 minutes, stirring occasionally. Add the shrimp and peas and simmer, covered, for another 10–12 minutes until the shrimp are cooked. Stir in a good knob of butter, parsley and parmesan cheese, if using, and serve immediately.

WHOLE SNAPPER WITH A MUSHROOM AND LEEK STUFFING

Serves 4

This is a great dish for a dinner party and looks good brought to the table on a platter.

Ingredients

- *90 g (3½ oz) quinoa grain, rinsed and drained*
- *240 ml (8 fl oz) water*
- *2 tbsp olive oil*
- *1 leek, washed and finely sliced*
- *250 g (8 oz) mushrooms, sliced*
- *salt and freshly ground black pepper*
- *2 large cloves garlic, finely chopped*
- *2 tbsp chopped flatleaf parsley*
- *1 tsp dried oregano leaves*
- *1 x 1.5 kg (3 lb) whole snapper, scaled and cleaned*
- *juice of 1 lemon*
- *extra virgin olive oil*
- *1 large tomato, sliced*
- *1 red onion, sliced*
- *2 scallions (spring onions), chopped*
- *1 tbsp chopped flatleaf parsley*

Preheat the oven to 185°C (360°F).

Place the quinoa in a small saucepan with the water. Bring to the boil, then reduce the heat, cover and simmer for 10 minutes until all the water is absorbed. Remove from the heat.

Heat the olive oil in a frying pan and sauté the leek until soft. Add the mushrooms, season with salt and pepper and cook until the mushrooms are soft. Stir in the garlic, then the parsley and oregano. Remove the pan from the heat, mix in the cooked quinoa and adjust the seasoning.

Place the fish on a large ovenproof lined with baking paper. Sprinkle the cavity of the fish with lemon juice and fill it with the stuffing. Pour remaining lemon juice over the fish, drizzle with extra virgin olive oil.

Place in the oven and bake for 15 minutes. Remove from the oven and arrange alternate slices of tomato and onion over the fish and sprinkle with the scallions and parsley. Loosely cover with foil, return to the oven and continue baking for another 30 minutes or until fish is cooked. Remove foil in the last 10 minutes or so of cooking to allow the tomatoes and onion to take on some color.

SUSHI

Makes 4 large sushi rolls

I find that white quinoa works best in this recipe.

Ingredients

- *185 g (6 oz) quinoa, rinsed and drained*
- *590 ml (20 fl oz) water*
- *1½ tbsp sugar*
- *2 tbsp rice wine vinegar*
- *4 nori sheets*
- *wasabi paste*
- *choice of fillings: fresh or tinned tuna, crab, shrimp (prawns), fresh salmon, cooked chicken, strips of cucumber, carrot, avocado, scallions (spring onions), bell pepper (capsicum)*

Place quinoa in a small saucepan with the water, bring to the boil, then reduce the heat, cover and simmer for 15 minutes until all the water is absorbed. The quinoa is cooked for a little longer in this dish as it needs to be a little gluggy.

Remove from the heat, stir in the sugar and vinegar and mix well—the quinoa should be quite sticky. Cool it a little.

Place the nori seaweed sheet, shiny side down, on a bamboo rolling mat.

Divide the quinoa into four and, using wet fingertips, spread evenly over the nori sheet leaving a 2½ cm (1 in) border at the end.

Dab a small amount of wasabi along the quinoa in a straight line at the edge closest to you. Place the fillings of your choice on top of the wasabi in a neat line.

Lift the bamboo mat at the closest edge to you and begin to slowly and tightly roll the nori sheet, at the same time separating the bamboo mat away from the rolled part of the nori sheet. Lightly wet the end of the sheet and gently press to join the edge together.

Using a wet serrated knife, slice the sushi in half or in 5–6 pieces.

STUFFED SQUID

Serves 4

Ingredients

- *4 cleaned large squid tubes*
- *185 g (6 oz) quinoa, rinsed and drained*
- *480 ml (16 fl oz) water*
- *2 tbsps extra virgin olive oil*
- *1 small onion, grated*
- *2 cloves garlic, grated*
- *2 fresh tomatoes, grated*
- *60 ml (2 fl oz) water*
- *2 tbsps chopped flat-leaf parsley*
- *salt and freshly cracked black pepper*
- *1 x 400 g (14 oz) can diced tomatoes*
- *2 cloves garlic, finely grated*
- *1 heaped tsp dried oregano leaves*
- *2 tbsps extra virgin olive oil*
- *salt and freshly cracked black pepper*
- *parsley, finely chopped, for garnish*

Method

To clean the squid, gently pull and separate the head from the hood. The insides should come away with the head including the ink sac. Remove the fine cartilage and gently pull away the very fine skin. The wings will come away with the skin. Cut out the eyes and remove the beak, which is in the centre of the tentacles, by pushing it up and away. Cut off a small piece at the base of the hood to allow water to freely run through and clean out anything that may be left behind. Rinse the cleaned calamari thoroughly in cold water.

Place quinoa in a small saucepan with the water. Bring to the boil, reduce the heat, cover and simmer for 10 minutes until all the water is absorbed.

In the meantime, heat the oil in a large frying pan and sauté the onion until golden, stir in the garlic and cook for 30 seconds.

Add the tomatoes with their juices, water and parsley, then season with salt and pepper. Cook for about 3–4 minutes until thick, then stir in the quinoa and allow to cool a little.

Fill each hood of the squid tube with the filling (try not to pack too tightly as the quinoa will continue to expand during baking) and secure the opening with a toothpick.

Preheat the oven to 190°C (375°F).

Mix together the canned tomatoes with the garlic, oregano and the extra virgin olive oil, and season with salt and pepper.

SALT AND PEPPER SQUID

Serves 6

Clean the squid by gently pulling and separating the head from the hood. Carefully remove and discard the ink sac and fine cartilage, then gently pull away the very fine dark skin. The wings will come away with the skin. Cut off a small piece at the base of the hood to allow water to freely run through and clean out anything that may be left behind. Rinse the cleaned squid thoroughly in cold water.

To clean the heads, remove the eyes and the thick membrane that is near them, by cutting them off just above the eye area.

Ready-cleaned squid is usually frozen and can be quite tough—buying it fresh and cleaning it yourself is preferable.

Ingredients

- *1 kg (2 lb 3 oz) whole squid*
- *250 g (9 oz) quinoa flour*
- *175 ml (6 fl oz) cold water*
- *2 tbsp crushed sea salt*
- *1 tbsp white pepper*
- *1 tbsp coarsely ground black pepper*
- *1–2 tsp chili flakes*
- *vegetable oil for deep-frying*
- *lemon wedges for serving*

Either buy ready-cleaned squid hoods or whole squid and clean them yourself, in which case you will have the tentacles to cook as well.

Slice the squid hood in half so it lays flat and, with a sharp knife, lightly score the inside part of the squid (without cutting right through) diagonally to form diamond shapes, then cut into thick strips. If you are using the tentacles, cut them in half.

Mix 75 g (3 oz) of flour with the water to form a paste. Mix together the remaining flour with the salt, white and black peppers and the chili flakes. (I suggest that you start with a lesser amount of salt and pepper, cook a couple of pieces to check and adjust your seasoning.)

Dip the squid pieces and tentacles into the batter, then into the flour mixture and deep-fry in hot oil until they curl, crisp up and turn golden brown. You may need to change the oil once during cooking. Drain on kitchen paper and serve hot with wedges of lemon.

SALMON WITH FENNEL AND TOMATOES

Serves 4–6

Ingredients

- *750 g (1 lb 10 oz) fresh salmon*
- *1 tbsp Dijon mustard*
- *1–2 tbsp lemon juice*
- *250 g (9 oz) grape or cherry tomatoes*
- *salt and freshly cracked pepper*
- *1 tbsp extra virgin olive oil*
- *2 tbsp extra virgin olive oil*
- *1 red onion, chopped*
- *2 cloves garlic, chopped*
- *1 tsp mustard seeds*
- *1 large fennel bulb, trimmed and sliced*
- *1 tbsp Dijon mustard, extra*
- *20 g (¾ oz) fresh dill, chopped*
- *275 g (10 oz) quinoa, rinsed and drained*
- *700 ml (24 fl oz) hot water*
- *salt and freshly cracked black pepper*
- *2 tbsp lemon juice*
- *dill, chopped, for garnish*

Preheat oven to 200°C (400°F) and line a baking tray with non-stick baking paper.

Make two to three incisions across each piece of salmon and rub in the mustard then sprinkle with lemon juice.

Place the salmon, skin side up, onto the baking tray and add the tomatoes. Season salmon and tomatoes with salt and pepper and drizzle with olive oil.

Bake for 15–18 minutes until salmon is cooked and tomatoes have collapsed. Remove from the oven, cool and flake the salmon into chunks with or without the skin.

In the meantime, heat oil in a large frying pan and sauté onion until lightly browned. Stir in the garlic and mustard seeds and cook for 1–2 minutes.

Add the fennel and cook for 4–5 minutes until soft, then stir in the mustard.

Stir in the dill, quinoa and water and season with salt and pepper. Bring to the boil, reduce the heat, cover and simmer for about 15 minutes until the quinoa is cooked and all the liquid is absorbed.

Gently toss the salmon and tomatoes through the quinoa, squeeze a good amount of lemon juice over the top and garnish with extra chopped dill.

SHRIMP WITH MANGO AND COCONUT QUINOA

Serves 4

Ingredients

- *275 g (10 oz) quinoa, rinsed and drained*
- *350 ml (12 fl oz) coconut milk*
- *350 ml (12 fl oz) water*
- *1 piece of lime rind*
- *2 tbsps oil*
- *2 large scallions (spring onions), finely chopped*
- *4 cloves garlic, finely chopped*
- *1–2 long red or green chilies, sliced*
- *750 g (12½ oz) green shrimp (prawns), peeled and de-veined*
- *Juice of 1 lime*
- *1 tbsp fish sauce*
- *120 ml (4 fl oz) warm water*
- *2 fresh mangoes, peeled and cubed*
- *Small handful cilantro (coriander) leaves, roughly chopped*
- *Salt and freshly cracked black pepper*
- *4 lime wedges, for serving*
- *Lime juice, extra, for serving*

Method

Place the quinoa in a medium saucepan with the coconut milk, water and the lime rind. Bring to the boil, reduce the heat, cover and simmer on low heat for about 12–15 minutes until all the liquid is absorbed. Leave to stand, covered, for 10 minutes while you prepare the shrimp.

Heat the oil in a large frying pan and sauté the scallions, garlic and chili until soft.

Stir in the shrimp and cook until they turn pink and are cooked.

Add the lime juice, fish sauce and water, and cook for 1–2 minutes.

Stir in the mangoes and cilantro, and cook until the mangoes are heated through and the sauce starts to thicken. Taste, then season with salt and pepper if you need to.

Fluff the quinoa with a fork and serve topped with the shrimp. Serve with a lime wedge and squeeze a little extra lime juice on top.

TUNA MORNAY WITH CRUNCHY TOPPING

Serves 4

This has been a regular dish in my family for years. I used to use wheat flour but swapped over to quinoa flour when I discovered it. It works just as well and you can't tell the difference at all. Everyone I have served this to absolutely loves it.

Ingredients

- *1 x 425 g (14½ oz) canned tuna in brine or spring water*
- *30 g (1 oz) butter*
- *3 tbsps quinoa flour*
- *1 tsp curry powder*
- *300 ml (10 fl oz) milk*
- *Salt and pepper*
- *90 g (3½ oz) tasty or mild cheese, grated*
- *90 g (3½ oz) cornflakes*
- *125 g (4½ oz) tasty or mild cheese, grated, extra*
- *1 tsp butter*

Preheat the oven to 180°C (350°F).

Drain and flake the tuna and place into a medium ovenproof casserole dish.

Melt the butter in a saucepan, then stir in the flour and curry powder to form a roux.

Slowly pour in the milk, stirring constantly until sauce starts to thicken and bubble. Season with salt and pepper then stir in the cheese and cook for about 2 minutes, until the cheese has melted into the sauce and the sauce is thick and bubbly.

Pour the sauce over tuna and mix thoroughly to combine.

In a separate bowl, lightly crush the cornflakes and mix with the extra cheese and sprinkle over the tuna. Dot with a little butter and place in the oven to bake for about 15–20 minutes or until topping is golden and crispy.

SMOKED SALMON PIZZA

Serves 2

Although not exactly the same as a regular pizza, this is a quick and easy way to make a gluten/wheat-free version. There is no kneading or resting of dough required and I like the nutty taste of this dough.

Ingredients

- *250 g (9 oz) quinoa flour*
- *1 tsp baking powder*
- *½ tsp baking soda (bicarbonate of soda)*
- *½ tsp ground oregano*
- *1 tsp garlic salt*
- *150 ml (5 fl oz) warm water (approx.)*
- *2 tbsps extra virgin olive oil*

TOPPING

- *1 small red onion, sliced thinly*
- *juice of ½ lime*
- *150 g (5 oz) cream cheese*
- *arugula (rocket) leaves*
- *150 g (5 oz) smoked salmon, thinly sliced*
- *250 g (9 oz) bocconcini cheese, torn into pieces*
- *2 tbsps capers*
- *extra virgin olive oil, for drizzling*
- *freshly cracked black pepper*

Preheat the oven to 200°C (400°F).

Sift flour into a bowl with the baking powder and baking soda, stir in the oregano and garlic salt, then make a well in the centre. Pour the water and oil in the well and with the tips of your fingers slowly incorporate the flour with the oil and water until the dough comes together and you have a workable dough that holds together. If the dough is too dry, add a little more water or vice versa.

Place the dough on a floured surface and shape into a flat disc. Place the disc onto a sheet of non-stick baking parchment/paper and roll out the pastry into a thin free form round or square shape, then place with the baking paper on a baking tray. (I find the pastry is much easier to handle and move around if on baking paper. You may find that the pastry may split along the edges as you roll it out: if that happens just pinch the sides together). Bake the pizza base for 15–20 minutes.

In the meantime, place the onion into a bowl with the lime juice and leave to stand for about 15 minutes.

Take the pizza out of the oven and spread with some cream cheese, then top with the arugula leaves, salmon, bocconcini (or bits of cream cheese) capers and the onion.

Drizzle a little extra virgin olive oil on top and sprinkle with lots of cracked pepper. Serve immediately.

SMOKED COD KEDGEREE

Serves 4

You can substitute the cod with fresh salmon. Poach the salmon as you would the cod.

Ingredients

- *275 g (10 oz) quinoa*
- *700 ml (24 fl oz) water*
- *750 g (1 lb 10 oz) smoked cod*
- *3 hard-boiled eggs*
- *1 tbsp butter*
- *2 tbsp extra virgin olive oil*
- *6 scallions (spring onions), sliced*
- *1 long red chili, sliced*
- *2 tsp curry paste or powder*
- *salt and freshly ground black pepper*
- *20 g (¾ oz) finely chopped flat-leaf parsley*
- *lemon juice, for serving*
- *parsley, chopped, for serving*

Method

Place quinoa in a small saucepan with the water, bring to the boil, then reduce the heat, cover and simmer for 10 minutes until all the water is absorbed. Remove from heat and cool completely.

Place the cod in a large frying pan with just enough water to cover. Bring to a simmering point, and then simmer, uncovered, for about 10 minutes until the fish is tender. Drain and reserve about 2 tbsps of the cooking liquid.

Remove and discard the skin and any bones from the fish and flake the flesh into large pieces. Peel and chop two of the eggs and slice the third.

Melt the butter and heat the oil in a large frying pan, add the scallions and chili and cook for 2–3 minutes until tender. Stir in the curry paste and reserved liquid and cook for 1–2 minutes.

Stir through the quinoa, coating completely in the curry. Add the fish and chopped egg, season with salt and pepper and gently toss to combine everything. Cook for about 3–5 minutes over gentle heat until heated through then stir in the parsley.

Place onto a serving platter, sprinkle with lemon juice and serve garnished with the sliced egg and extra parsley.

Sweet Things

BLUEBERRY FRIANDS

Makes 9 friands

You can substitute raspberries or blackberries for the blueberries if you prefer.

Ingredients

- *125 g (4 oz) almond meal*
- *130 g (4½ oz) confectioners' (icing) sugar, sifted*
- *60 g (2 oz) quinoa flour*
- *125 g (4 oz) unsalted butter, melted and cooled*
- *½ tsp vanilla extract*
- *4 large egg whites*
- *250 g (8 oz) fresh blueberries*

Preheat the oven to 170°C (325°F). Grease a 9-cup friand tin with butter.

Place the almond meal, confectioners' sugar and quinoa flour in a bowl. Using a whisk, mix well, breaking up any lumps of mixture that may form. Lightly mix in the melted butter and vanilla extract.

Beat the egg whites until foamy and soft peaks form, and gently fold into the mixture.

Spoon the mixture into the prepared tin. Place 5–6 blueberries around the centre of each friand and lightly press them down into the mixture.

Bake for about 25 minutes, until lightly browned and cooked when a metal skewer comes out clean.

STICKY DATE PUDDINGS WITH CARAMEL SAUCE

Makes 12 individual puddings

I prefer to make this recipe as little individual puddings—they are a nice serving size—and have always done so as I like the look of them when served. Also they cook a lot quicker. You can, of course, make one large pudding if you prefer, just vary the cooking time.

Ingredients

- *500 g (17½ oz) dried dates*
- *590 ml (20 fl oz) water*
- *1 tsp baking soda (bicarbonate of soda)*
- *250 g (9 oz) unsalted butter*
- *250 g (9 oz) superfine (caster) sugar*
- *4 extra large eggs*
- *2 tsp vanilla extract*
- *1 tsp ground cinnamon*
- *250 g (9 oz) quinoa flour*
- *2 tsp baking powder*
- *strawberries, for garnish*

CARAMEL SAUCE

- *200 g (7 oz) unsalted butter*
- *400 g (14 oz) brown sugar*
- *240 ml (8 fl oz) pouring cream*
- *1 tsp vanilla extract*

Method

Place dates and water into a large saucepan and bring slowly to the boil, reduce the heat and simmer for 1 minute. Remove from heat, stir in the baking soda and set aside to cool. The whole mixture will froth up when you add the soda so make sure you use a big enough saucepan so it doesn't spill over and don't worry about all the liquid left as the date mixture will thicken as it cools.

Preheat oven to 160°C (325°F) and grease 12 1-cup capacity tin moulds. Using electric beaters, cream the butter and sugar together until light. Beat in the eggs, one at a time, with the vanilla and cinnamon.

Sift the flour and baking powder and slowly incorporate with the creamed butter mixture. Fold in the cooled dates and divide cake mixture evenly between the prepared tins. Place tins on a baking tray and bake for 35–40 minutes. When cooled, run a thin knife along the side of the moulds to loosen the puddings, then invert onto a serving plate and serve with lots of caramel sauce and a fanned strawberry.

To make the caramel sauce, place all ingredients into a small saucepan and simmer for a few minutes until the sauce starts to bubble and thicken.

PISTACHIO BISCUITS

Makes 20–24

These biscuits are so easy to make and are very popular in our household. I often have to make a double quantity as they just disappear and don't stay long enough in the container. They are great for school lunches or picnics or just to take to somebody's house.

Ingredients

- *125 g (4½ oz) quinoa flour*
- *1½ tsps baking powder*
- *1 tsp baking soda (bicarbonate of soda)*
- *80 g (3 oz) quinoa flakes*
- *125 g (4 oz) shelled, unsalted pistachio nuts, chopped but not too finely*
- *190 g (6½ oz) superfine (caster) sugar*
- *150 g (5 oz) unsalted butter, melted*
- *1 tsp vanilla bean paste or extract*
- *1 extra large egg, lightly beaten*

Method

Preheat the oven to 180°C (350°F) and line two baking trays with non-stick baking parchment/paper.

Sift the flour, baking powder and baking soda into a bowl, then stir in the quinoa flakes, chopped pistachio nuts and sugar.

Pour in the melted butter and vanilla, mix well, then stir in the egg and mix everything together until you have a mixture that holds together when pressed between your fingertips.

Take spoonfuls of the mixture, the size of a walnut, and lightly roll into a ball then place onto the prepared trays and lightly flatten.

The biscuits will spread during baking so leave enough space between each one on the tray.

Bake for 10–12 minutes until golden. Cool completely on the trays before removing and storing in an airtight container. Biscuits are crisp on the outside and chewy on the inside.

These biscuits keep well in an airtight container.

ORANGE AND MIXED BERRY TARTS

Makes 8

These little tarts are best eaten on the day they are made. They are lovely served as a dinner party dessert with some good vanilla ice cream or custard. You can use whatever berries you like, either frozen or fresh. I have used frozen purely for convenience sake, so you can make these little tarts at anytime of the year.

Ingredients

- *250 g (9 oz) frozen mixed berries*
- *185 g (6½ oz) quinoa flour*
- *1 tsp baking powder*
- *60 g (2½ oz) ground almond meal*
- *95 g (3½ oz) superfine (caster) sugar*
- *1 extra large egg*
- *150 ml (5 fl oz) milk*
- *1 tsp vanilla*
- *60 g (2 oz) butter, melted*
- *zest of 1 orange*
- *juice of half an orange*
- *zest of 1 orange, for topping*
- *3 tbsps superfine (caster) sugar, for topping*

Method

Remove the berries from the freezer. Place them in a colander and set aside to partially thaw as you prepare the other ingredients.

Preheat the oven to 170°C (325°F) and grease eight round 10 x 2 cm (4 x ¾ in) tart tins with butter.

Sift the quinoa flour and baking powder together and combine with the almond meal and sugar in a large bowl. In another bowl, whisk together the egg, milk, vanilla and butter, then stir in the orange zest and juice.

Pour the wet ingredients into the dry ingredients and, using a spatula, gently mix until well combined.

Pour the mixture evenly between tins, filling about three-quarters full. Gently tap the tins on your kitchen bench to remove any air bubbles.

Scatter the berries on top and use your fingertips to rub together the extra zest with the extra sugar and sprinkle on top of each tart.

Bake for about 25–30 minutes.

Leave to stand in the tins for 5–10 minutes before carefully removing the tarts from the tins and cooling on a wire rack.

CHOCOLATE BITES

Makes about 30 pieces

These are a lovely special treat that everyone in the family can enjoy. You can add a few drops of peppermint essence for a twist on the after-dinner mint or, if making these for adults only, add 1–2 tbsps of your favorite liquor.

Ingredients

- *60 g (2½ oz) quinoa flakes*
- *200 g (7 oz) dark chocolate, chopped*
- *100 g (3½ oz) milk chocolate, chopped*
- *125 g (4 oz) butter*
- *1 tsp vanilla extract*
- *2 tbsps golden syrup*
- *185 g (6 oz) Toasted Quinoa (see recipe page 27)*
- *60 g (2 oz) flaked almonds*

Lightly toast the quinoa flakes in a medium- to large-sized non-stick frying pan over a low-medium heat. You need a pan that has enough surface space for the flakes to toast as evenly as possible. Keep an eye on the flakes by regularly moving them around the pan as they can burn very easily. Once they turn a light golden color—you will be able to smell them at this point—remove from the heat and transfer the toasted flakes into a dish to cool completely.

Line a 20 cm (8 in) baking tray with aluminium foil and set aside.

Place the chocolate, butter, vanilla and golden syrup into a medium-sized saucepan and stir over low heat until the chocolate and butter have melted.

Stir in the toasted quinoa, cooled quinoa flakes and almonds then pour the chocolate mixture into the prepared tin.

Refrigerate overnight or until set into a firm consistency, then cut into bite-sized pieces to serve.

Store these chocolate bites in the refrigerator at all times in a covered container.

FRUIT AND NUT SLICE

Makes 16

Ingredients

- *250 g (9 oz) dried figs, finely chopped*
- *Juice and grated rind of 1 large orange*
- *3 tbsps water*
- *125 g (4½ oz) quinoa flour*
- *80 g (3 oz) quinoa flakes*
- *50 g (2 oz) granulated/raw sugar*
- *1 tsp baking powder*
- *1 tsp ground cinnamon*
- *1 extra large egg*
- *150 g (5 oz) unsalted butter, melted*
- *60 g (3 oz) walnuts, finely chopped*
- *1 extra large egg (extra)*
- *1 extra large egg white*
- *1 tsp vanilla bean paste*
- *125 g (4 oz) coconut flakes*

Method

Preheat the oven to 180°C (350°F) and line a 18 x 29 cm (7 x 11½ in) slice tin with non-stick baking parchment/paper, letting some hang over the sides.

Place the figs, orange juice, orange rind and water into a small saucepan and cook, covered, over low heat for about 10 minutes until figs soften and are almost sticky.

Mix together the flour, flakes, sugar, baking powder and cinnamon until combined. Stir in the egg and melted butter until the mixture is combined. It should be moist and hold together.

Press the mixture firmly into the base of a prepared tin and bake for 15 minutes. Remove from the oven and spread the fig mixture on top, then sprinkle the walnuts over the figs.

Whisk together the extra egg, egg white and vanilla, then stir in the coconut. Using a fork, spread this mixture over the figs and walnuts. Place the tin in the oven and bake for 25–30 minutes until golden.

Cool in the tin until barely warm, then remove and cut into squares. Alternatively, you could cut into larger squares then halve the squares into triangles.

STEAMED CHRISTMAS FRUIT PUDDING

Serves 8

Ingredients

- *60 g (2½ oz) quinoa flour*
- *½ tsp baking soda (bicarbonate of soda)*
- *½ tsp gluten-free baking powder*
- *1 heaped tsp ground cinnamon*
- *2 tsp mixed spice*
- *pinch of salt*
- *60 g (2½ oz) quinoa flakes*
- *200 g (7 oz) brown sugar, tightly packed*
- *675 g (23½ oz) mixed fruit*
- *50 g (1¾ oz) mixed peel*
- *50 g (1¾ oz) flaked almonds, chopped*
- *grated zest of 1 lemon*
- *grated zest of 1 orange*
- *3 tbsp orange juice*
- *2 tbsp treacle*
- *2–3 tbsp brandy*
- *2 extra large eggs, lightly beaten*
- *125 g (4 oz) butter, melted*

Grease an 2–2½ litre pudding basin with butter.

Sift together the flour, baking soda, baking powder, cinnamon, mixed spice and salt.

Mix in the quinoa flakes, sugar, mixed fruit (break up any lumps of fruit that may have stuck together), mixed peel, almonds, lemon and orange zest, orange juice, treacle and brandy. Add the eggs and butter and stir well until evenly mixed.

Pour mixture into the prepared basin, pushing down well into the basin and flatten the top with the back of a spoon.

Loosely cover the top of the pudding with a sheet of non-stick baking paper then cover the top of the basin with plastic wrap. Secure by using an elastic band to hold the plastic wrap in place.

Fill a large saucepan with enough hot water to come halfway up the side of the pudding basin and carefully place the pudding into the saucepan.

Reduce heat to a low simmer, cover saucepan with a lid and cook pudding for about 3 hours. Remove from the saucepan and allow to cool in the pudding basin.

Gently run a thin knife along the inside of the basin to release the pudding then invert on to serving platter and serve with brandy custard. You can serve the pudding cold or warm by re-heating in microwave. It can be prepared up to 4–6 weeks before serving.

APPLE PUDDING

Serves 6

Ingredients

- *5 large cooking apples, peeled, cored and sliced*
- *100 g (3½ oz) brown sugar*
- *grated rind of 1 lemon*
- *1 tbsp lemon juice*
- *60 ml (2 fl oz) water*
- *75 g (2½ oz) butter at room temperature*
- *95 g (3½ oz) superfine (caster) sugar*
- *1 tsp vanilla bean paste or extract*
- *2 extra large eggs*
- *125 g (4½ oz) quinoa flour*
- *½ tsp baking powder*
- *½ tsp baking soda (bicarbonate of soda)*
- *30 g (1 oz) almond meal*
- *3 tbsps milk*
- *90 g (3 oz) flaked almonds*
- *custard, for serving*

Preheat the oven to 180°C (350°F) and lightly grease a deep 2-litre (64 fl oz) ovenproof dish with butter.

Mix the apples with the brown sugar, lemon rind, juice and water in a saucepan and bring to the boil. Cover and simmer for about 7–10 minutes or until the apples are tender.

In the meantime, cream the butter, superfine sugar and vanilla until light and creamy. Add the eggs and mix well.

Sift in the flour, baking powder and baking soda, and, using a spatula, fold into the egg mixture, together with the almond meal and milk.

As soon as the apples are tender, place them into the prepared dish while they are still hot and drop spoonfuls of the flour mixture on top.

Sprinkle the flaked almonds on top and bake for about 20–25 minutes until the sponge and almonds are golden.

Serve warm or cold with custard.

PINEAPPLE, BANANA AND WALNUT CAKE

Serves 8–10

Ingredients

- *185 g (6½ oz) quinoa flour*
- *250 g (9 oz) superfine (caster) sugar*
- *1 tsp ground cinnamon*
- *3 eggs, lightly beaten*
- *175 ml (6 fl oz) vegetable oil or extra light olive oil*
- *450 g (1 lb) can crushed pineapple, with juice*
- *3 medium ripe bananas, mashed*
- *90 g (3 oz) crushed walnuts or pecans, plus extra for decorating*
- *1 tsp vanilla extract*

FROSTING

- *3 tbsp soft cream cheese*
- *2 tbsp soft unsalted butter*
- *1 tsp vanilla essence*
- *195 g (7 oz) confectioners' (icing) sugar, sifted*

Preheat the oven to 175°C (340°F). Butter a 23 cm (9 in) square cake tin, preferably non-stick, line the bottom with baking paper; lightly butter the paper.

Sift the quinoa flour, sugar and cinnamon into a large bowl. Fold in the eggs, oil, pineapple and juice, bananas, nuts and vanilla. Stir until just combined.

Pour the cake mixture into the prepared cake tin and bake for 1–1¼ hours, until cooked. The cake should be golden and firm to the touch and a skewer should come out clean when inserted. Stand the cake in the tin for 10 minutes before turning onto a wire rack to cool.

To make the frosting, beat the cream cheese, butter and vanilla together, then slowly mix in the sifted confectioners' sugar. Ice the cake with the frosting when completely cold and decorate with extra nuts.

CHOCOLATE CAKE

Serves 6

This cake remains moist and lasts for a few days.

Ingredients

- *1 tsp instant coffee powder*
- *1 tsp hot water*
- *4 eggs*
- *145 g (5 oz) superfine (caster) sugar*
- *1 tsp vanilla extract*
- *150 g (5 oz) dark chocolate*
- *60 g (2½ oz) quinoa flour*

ICING

- *4 tbsp cocoa powder, sifted*
- *75 g (3 oz) melted butter*
- *390 g (13½ oz) confectioners' (icing) sugar, sifted*
- *3 tbsp hot water*

Method

Preheat the oven to 160°C (310°F).

Butter 2 x 20 cm (8 in) round cake tins and line the bottoms with baking paper; lightly butter the paper.

Dissolve the coffee in the hot water. Beat the eggs and sugar with an electric beater until light and fluffy, stir in the vanilla and the dissolved coffee.

Melt the chocolate in a bowl over hot simmering water, making sure that the bowl does not come in contact with the water. Cool slightly.

Mix the chocolate into the egg mixture, then fold in the flour. Divide the mixture equally between the two cake tins and bake for about 15 minutes. Remove from the oven and leave in the tins for 5–10 minutes before turning out onto a wire rack to cool.

Prepare the icing by placing the cocoa in a bowl, stir in the butter and then the confectioners' sugar, then add enough hot water to mix into a smooth spreading consistency.

When the cake is cold, sandwich the two halves together with a good layer of icing, then cover cake completely with the remaining icing. Decorate as desired.

CARROT CAKE WITH CREAM CHEESE FROSTING

Serves 8–10

Ingredients

- *185 g (6½ oz) quinoa flour*
- *1½ tsp baking soda (bicarbonate of soda)*
- *1½ tsp gluten-free baking powder*
- *1½ tsp ground cinnamon*
- *pinch of salt*
- *3 extra large eggs*
- *190 g (6½ oz) superfine (caster) sugar*
- *2 tsp vanilla extract*
- *175 ml (6 fl oz) extra light olive oil or vegetable oil*
- *100g (3½ oz) raw carrot, grated*
- *60 g (2½ oz) walnuts, finely chopped*
- *walnut halves, for decoration*
- *ground cinnamon, for decoration*

CREAM CHEESE FROSTING

- *125 g (4 oz) cream cheese, at room temperature*
- *3 tbsp butter, softened*
- *250 g (9 oz) pure confectioners' (icing) sugar, sifted*
- *1½ tsp vanilla extract*

Preheat oven to 160°C (325°F) and grease a 24 cm (9½ in) non-stick, square tin.

Sift together the flour, baking soda, baking powder, cinnamon and salt.

Using electric beaters, beat the eggs, sugar and vanilla until light and fluffy then mix in the oil. Stir in the dry ingredients then fold in the carrot and walnuts. Pour into the prepared tin and bake for about 45 minutes or until a skewer comes out clean when tested.

Remove from oven and cool in the tin for about 15 minutes then turn out onto a wire rack to cool completely. When cooled, ice the top of the cake with cream cheese frosting, decorate with extra walnuts and sprinkle with cinnamon powder. I like to refrigerate the cake after icing for about half an hour to allow the icing to set.

To make the frosting, using an electric mixer, combine cream cheese, butter, confectioners' sugar and vanilla. Beat until light and fluffy.

SPICED TEA CAKE

Serves 6-8

I love the smell of the spices wafting through the house as this cake is baking. You can serve it warm or cold, and it is lovely with a hot cup of tea or coffee.

Ingredients

- *185 g (6½ oz) quinoa flour*
- *1½ tsp gluten-free baking powder*
- *1½ tsp baking soda (bicarbonate of soda)*
- *2 tsps ground cinnamon*
- *1 tsp ground allspice*
- *½ tsp ground nutmeg*
- *125 g (4 oz) butter*
- *1 tsp vanilla bean paste or extract*
- *190 g (6½ oz) superfine (caster) sugar*
- *2 extra large eggs*
- *75 ml (2½ fl oz) milk*
- *confectioners' (icing) sugar, for dusting*
- *cream, for serving*
- *cinnamon, for sprinkling*

Preheat the oven to 160°C (325°F) and grease a 20 cm (8 in) non-stick cake tin.

Sift together the flour, baking powder, baking soda, cinnamon, allspice and nutmeg.

Using electric beaters, cream the butter, vanilla and sugar together until creamy. Add the eggs one at a time, and beat until light and fluffy.

Using a spatula, fold in the flour alternately with the milk then pour the mixture into the prepared tin. Bake for approximately 30–35 minutes or until skewer comes out clean when tested. Remove the cake from the oven and leave to stand for about 15 minutes before removing from tin and slicing.

Dust the cake with confectioners' sugar and serve warm with a dollop of cream with a little cinnamon sprinkled on top.

RASPBERRY MUFFINS

Makes 12

You can replace the raspberries with any other frozen berries. Muffins are lovely eaten warm or cold and these ones will remain fresh and moist for three to four days.

Ingredients

- *250 g (9 oz) quinoa flour*
- *250 g (9 oz) superfine (caster) sugar*
- *1 level tsp baking soda (bicarbonate of soda)*
- *⅛ tsp salt*
- *240 ml (8 fl oz) milk*
- *2 large eggs*
- *1½ tsp vanilla paste or extract*
- *75 ml (2½ fl oz) vegetable oil*
- *175 g (6 oz) frozen raspberries*

Preheat the oven to 180°C (350°F) and line a 12-cup muffin tin with 12 paper cases.

Sift together the flour, sugar, baking soda and salt into a large bowl. Pour the milk into a jug, then lightly beat in the eggs, vanilla and oil.

Make a well in the centre of the dry ingredients and slowly pour in the liquid ingredients, mixing as you go until all the ingredients are combined. Gently fold in the frozen raspberries; do not over mix.

Spoon the mixture into the prepared muffin tin and bake for 30–35 minutes until the muffins have risen, are golden, firm to the touch and a skewer comes out clean when inserted into a muffin.

Leave to rest in the tin for 10–15 minutes before serving warm or placing on a wire rack to cool.

APPLE AND CINNAMON BUTTERMILK PANCAKES

Makes 8–10 pancakes

The buttermilk makes the pancakes light and fluffy. They are best eaten as soon as they are cooked—they are delicious as they are or with a drizzle of maple sugar or a light dusting of confectioners' sugar. Make sure to use a sweet-tasting apple—it really makes a difference.

Ingredients

- *1 large egg*
- *95 g (3½ oz) superfine (caster) sugar*
- *1 tsp ground cinnamon*
- *1 tsp vanilla extract*
- *240 ml (8 fl oz) buttermilk*
- *125 g (4½ oz) quinoa flour*
- *1 large sweet apple, unpeeled and coarsely grated (I prefer red delicious)*
- *unsalted butter for cooking*

Whisk the egg and sugar together until light, then mix in the cinnamon and vanilla. Whisk in the buttermilk until combined, then slowly mix in the flour a little at a time until you get a smooth, lump-free mixture. Fold in the grated apple.

Heat a small non-stick frying pan until hot and add a little butter. When melted, pour in small ladlefuls of pancake mixture. Swirl the pan around to form an even pancake and cook on both sides until golden. Serve immediately.

TIRAMISU

Serves 8–10

Ingredients

- 2 tbsp instant coffee
- 2 tbsp boiling water
- 185 g (6½ oz) quinoa flour
- 1½ tsp gluten-free baking powder
- 1½ tsp baking soda (bicarbonate of soda)
- 1 tbsp cocoa powder
- 125 g (4 oz) butter, softened
- 2 tsp vanilla extract
- 95 g (3½ oz) superfine (caster) sugar
- 2 extra large eggs
- 120 ml (4 fl oz) milk

FILLING

- 500 g (17½ oz) mascarpone cheese
- 3–4 tbsp confectioners' (icing) sugar
- 2 tsp vanilla extract
- zest and juice of 1 large orange
- 120 ml (4 fl oz) milk
- 1 x 670 g (23½ oz) jar of cherries in syrup
- cocoa powder, for garnish
- chocolate shavings, for garnish
- 1 quantity coffee cake

To make the coffee cake, preheat the oven to 160°C (325°F) and grease a 20 cm (8 in) non-stick square cake tin.

Dissolve the coffee in the boiling water and set aside. Sift quinoa flour, baking powder, baking soda and cocoa together.

Cream butter, vanilla and sugar together until creamy, add the eggs one at a time and beat until light and fluffy. Stir in half the flour with the coffee and half the milk. Add remaining flour and milk and beat until mixture is smooth. Pour into prepared tin and bake for approx. 25 minutes or until skewer comes out clean when tested. Leave in the tin for 15 minutes before turning out on to a rack to cool.

To make the filling, mix together the mascarpone, confectioners' sugar, vanilla, orange zest and juice and the milk until you have a smooth and creamy mixture. Drain the cherries and reserve some of the liquid.

To assemble, crumble half the coffee cake into the bottom of a glass serving bowl and sprinkle with about 4–5 tbsps of the reserved syrup. Top with half the cherries and half the mascarpone mixture.

Repeat this process, finishing off with a layer of the mascarpone mixture. Sprinkle the top with cocoa and decorate with the chocolate shavings. Refrigerate overnight before serving.

CREAMY COCONUT AND MANGO PUDDING

Serves 6–8

To toast the coconut flakes, place into a small non-stick frying pan and toast over a low heat—there's no need to add any oil or butter. This pudding is a favorite with everyone—it's absolutely delicious.

Ingredients

- *140 g (5 oz) quinoa grain, rinsed and drained*
- *2 x 400 g (14 oz) cans coconut milk, plus extra 120 ml (4 fl oz)*
- *150 g (5 oz) sugar*
- *2 fresh mangoes*
- *40 g (1½ oz) toasted coconut flakes*

Method

Place the quinoa in a large saucepan with all the coconut milk and the sugar. Bring to the boil, then reduce the heat, cover and simmer on low heat for 20–25 minutes, until thick and creamy.

Meanwhile, peel the mangoes. Thinly slice half of one to use as decoration later; set aside. Cut remaining mangoes into small pieces.

When the quinoa is soft and cooked, stir through the mango pieces and pour into individual bowls or a large serving bowl. Sprinkle with the toasted coconut and decorate with the slices of mango. Refrigerate before serving.

PEAR CLAFOUTIS

Serves 6

This is a light dessert and is best eaten while still warm. It is delicious any time of the year with cream or ice cream.

Ingredients

- *4 large ripe pears*
- *60 g (2 oz) butter, melted*
- *4 eggs*
- *95 g (3½ oz) sugar, plus 2 tbsp*
- *1 tsp vanilla bean paste or extract*
- *90 g (3½ oz) quinoa flour*
- *480 ml (16 fl oz) full-fat milk*
- *½ tsp nutmeg*
- *confectioners' (icing) sugar for dusting*

Preheat the oven to 185°C (350°F).

Peel and core the pears, then thinly slice.

Use a little of the melted butter to grease a deep ovenproof tart dish, then pour the remaining butter over the pears and toss gently to coat each slice. Arrange the pear slices decoratively over the base of the dish. If you have extra slices just overlap them.

Beat the eggs and sugar with an electric beater until light and creamy, then stir in vanilla. Slowly add the flour and milk and continue mixing until combined.

Pour the mixture over the pears, sprinkle with nutmeg and bake for about 1–1¼ hours, until set and firm to the touch in the centre. Rest for 5–10 minutes before dusting with confectioners' sugar and serving.

CHOCOLATE, SEEDS AND NUT SNACK BARS

Makes about 20

I love the look of whole peanuts through these bars, however, if they are too big, they can be a bit difficult to cut so a rough chop is not a bad idea. You can also replace the peanuts with other nuts or leave them out altogether. These bars are great when you need a quick snack.

Ingredients

- *90 g (3½ oz) quinoa flour*
- *1 tsp gluten-free baking powder*
- *80 g (3 oz) quinoa flakes*
- *200 g (7 oz) brown sugar*
- *125 g (4 oz) chocolate chips, dark or milk*
- *125 g (4 oz) raw or roasted peanuts, roughly chopped (see note)*
- *60 g (2 oz) blanched, slivered almonds*
- *125 g (4 oz) pepitas/pumpkin seeds*
- *125 g (4 oz) sunflower seeds*
- *60 g (2 oz) butter, melted*
- *1 tsp vanilla bean paste*
- *2 extra large eggs, lightly beaten*
- *chocolate chips, extra*

Method

Preheat the oven to 180°C (350°F) and lightly grease a 29 x 19 cm (12 x 7½ in) slice tin then line with baking parchment/paper. Greasing the tin first helps the parchment stay in place.

Sift the flour and baking powder into a large bowl then stir in the quinoa flakes and sugar; mix well, making sure you break up any lumps in the sugar.

Add the chocolate chips, peanuts, almonds, pepitas and sunflower seeds and mix well to combine everything together.

Pour the melted butter, vanilla and the eggs over the flour mixture and stir really well until everything is combined and not dry. Evenly distribute the butter and egg throughout the flour mixture.

Using the back of a spoon, press the mix firmly into the prepared tin. Scatter as many of the extra chocolate chips over the top as you like, and bake for about 20–25 minutes until golden.

Remove from the oven and leave to cool in the tin for about 15 minutes and then cut into desired sized bars. Leave to cool in the tin for a little longer, then carefully remove the slice with the paper and place on a cooling rack to cool completely.

PLUM TART

Serves 6–8

The tart is best served on the day it is made. You can chop the walnuts, then prepare the pastry dough in a food processor or a mixer, using a plastic blade. If you use steel blades, the walnuts will be too finely chopped.

If plums are not in season, you can use 2 x 800 g (28 oz) cans of plums, drained well.

Ingredients

- *125 g (4 oz) walnuts*
- *250 g (9 oz) quinoa flour*
- *200 g (7 oz) brown sugar, tightly packed*
- *2 tsp vanilla extract*
- *185 g (7 oz) unsalted butter*
- *1 large egg yolk*
- *8 ripe plums, stoned, quartered*
- *confectioners' (icing) sugar for dusting (optional)*

Preheat the oven to 170°C (325°F). Butter a 24 cm (9½ in) loose-bottom tart tin.

Finely chop the walnuts and place in a large mixing bowl. Add the flour, sugar, vanilla and mix well. Rub in the butter until the mixture starts coming together, then mix in the egg yolk. The dough should resemble a crumble mixture but hold together when pressed in your hand. Take out about 60 g (2 oz) of the pastry and set aside.

Press the remaining dough tightly into the bottom and sides of the prepared tin. Arrange the plums, skin side down, decoratively over the base of the tart. Sprinkle the reserved walnut mixture over the top of the plums and bake for 30–40 minutes, until golden. Cool in the tin before gently loosening the sides and removing the tart from the tin. Sprinkle with confectioners' sugar before serving if you wish.

CHOCOLATE AND ORANGE SOUFFLÉ

Serves 4

Ingredients

- *95 g (3½ oz) superfine (caster) sugar*
- *3 extra large eggs, separated*
- *1 extra large egg, whole*
- *4 tbsps quinoa flour*
- *350 ml (11½ fl oz) milk*
- *200 g (7 oz) dark chocolate, broken into small pieces*
- *zest and juice 1 large orange*
- *½ tsp instant coffee*
- *confectioners' (icing sugar), for dusting*
- *fresh raspberries or strawberries for serving*

Method

Preheat the oven to 180°C (350°F) and grease 4 x 240 ml (8 fl oz) capacity ramekins with butter.

Cream the sugar, egg yolks and the 1 whole egg until pale and creamy.

Stir in the flour then pour in the milk and whisk until smooth.

Transfer to a saucepan and bring to the boil over a low heat, stirring constantly until the mixture thickens.

Break the chocolate into small pieces; add to the custard with the orange juice, zest and coffee. Take the mixture off the heat and stir until the chocolate melts.

In a clean bowl, whisk the egg whites until stiff, and gently fold into the chocolate mixture.

Pour the mixture into the prepared ramekins, then run your finger tip along the inside and top of the rim of each ramekin to separate the mixture from the dish so that the soufflé will rise more during baking.

Bake for about 30–35 minutes until the soufflés have risen and are firm to the touch.

Dust with confectioners' sugar and serve immediately with some fresh raspberries or strawberries on the side of the dish.

SOUR CREAM LEMON CHEESECAKE

Serves 6-8

Traditionally a cheesecake is made with a biscuit base. The base in this recipe is made using quinoa flour and flakes, which makes it gluten/wheat-free and delicious. Don't be concerned if the cheesecake splits after baking—they sometimes do that.

Ingredients

- *125 g (4½ oz) quinoa flour*
- *80 g (3 oz) quinoa flakes*
- *50 g (2 oz) raw sugar*
- *1 tsp baking powder*
- *1 teaspooon ground cinnamon*
- *150 g (5 oz) unsalted butter, melted*
- *500 g (17½ oz) cream cheese, at room temperature*
- *240 ml (8 fl oz) sour cream*
- *3 extra large eggs*
- *190 g (6½ oz) superfine (caster) sugar*
- *zest of 1 lemon*
- *4 tbsps lemon juice*
- *1 tsp vanilla bean paste or extract*
- *fresh whipped cream, for serving*
- *fresh strawberries, for garnish*

Preheat the oven to 180°C (350°F).

Mix together the flour, flakes, sugar, baking powder and cinnamon until combined. Stir in the melted butter and mix until well combined and moist, and holds together.

Grease and line the base of a 20 cm (8 in) round non-stick springform tin. Press the mixture firmly into the base of the tin and bake for 15 minutes. Remove from the oven and reduce the oven temperature to 160°C (325°F).

Place a small ovenproof bowl of hot water on the bottom rack of the oven. This will provide moisture during the baking time so the cheesecake won't dry out.

Place the cream cheese, sour cream, eggs, sugar, lemon zest, lemon juice and vanilla into a food processor and process until smooth. Don't over-mix.

Pour the cheese mixture onto the crumb base and bake for about 50–55 minutes until the cheesecake is cooked. Cheesecake is ready when the edges are slightly puffed and the centre is slightly wobbly. Cool for at least 30 minutes, then refrigerate for several hours before serving.

Remove from the tin and decorate with whipped cream and fresh strawberries to serve.

APRICOT AND COCONUT SLICE

Makes 16 pieces

This slice keeps well in an airtight container for two to three weeks, although it is usually eaten long before that.

Ingredients

- *60 g (2½ oz) quinoa flour*
- *1 tsp gluten-free baking powder*
- *80 g (3 oz) quinoa flakes*
- *75 g (3 oz) shredded coconut*
- *150 g (5 oz) raw (Demerara/turbinado) sugar*
- *200 g (7 oz) dried apricots, chopped*
- *150 g (5 oz) butter, melted*

Preheat oven to 180°C (350°F).

Sift flour and baking powder into a large bowl. Add the quinoa flakes, coconut, sugar and the chopped apricots. Stir in the melted butter and mix thoroughly to combine. Make sure all the ingredients are completely coated with the butter.

Press the apricot mixture firmly into an ungreased, non-stick 27 x 17 cm (10½ x 6½ in) slice tin.

Bake for 20–25 minutes or until a golden brown color.

Remove from the oven, cool for 5 minutes and, while still warm, cut into 16 pieces, then cool completely in the tin before storing in an airtight container.

LIME TART

Serves 6

This is another family favorite and I'm sure it will become one of yours too.

Ingredients

- *125 g (4½ oz) quinoa flour*
- *1 tsp gluten-free baking powder*
- *1 tsp baking soda (bicarbonate of soda)*
- *95 g (3½ oz) superfine (caster) sugar*
- *60 g (2 oz) butter*
- *1 extra large egg*
- *1 tsp vanilla extract*
- *confectioners' (icing) sugar, for dusting*

FILLING

- *60 g (2 oz) butter*
- *60 ml (2 fl oz) lime juice*
- *95 g (3½ oz) sugar*
- *1 extra large egg*

Method

Preheat oven to 170°C (335°F) and brush a round 20 x 4 cm (8 x 1½ in) non-stick cake tin with butter and line the base of the tin with non-stick baking paper.

Sift the flour, baking powder and baking soda into a bowl, add sugar and stir well to combine.

Using your fingertips, rub the butter into the flour until the mixture resembles fine breadcrumbs.

Lightly whisk the egg with the vanilla extract then stir into the flour mixture until you get a soft dough that holds together.

Using your fingers, press two-thirds of the dough into the base of the baking tin allowing the dough to come halfway up the sides of the tin. Pour the hot filling into the tin.

Take pieces of the remaining pastry and press between your fingertips to form small discs the size of a small coin and place over filling.

Bake for about 25 minutes until the top is golden. Cool completely in the tin before transferring to a serving platter. Dust with confectioners' sugar before serving.

To make the filling, combine all ingredients in a small saucepan and stir constantly over low heat until mixture starts to bubble and thicken.

CHOCOLATE CHIP COOKIES ON A STICK

Makes about 15 cookies

If making for gluten/wheat intolerant people, chocolate chips should be checked that they are wheat/gluten free.

Ingredients

- *185 g (6½ oz) quinoa flour*
- *1 tsp gluten-free baking powder*
- *½ tsp baking soda (bicarbonate of soda)*
- *¼ tsp salt*
- *180 g (6 oz) chocolate chips*
- *125 g (4 oz) butter, softened*
- *50 g (2 oz) brown sugar*
- *95 g (3½ oz) superfine (caster) sugar*
- *2 tsp vanilla extract*
- *2 extra large eggs*
- *wooden ice-cream/lollipop sticks*

Method

Preheat the oven to 180°C (350°F) and line two baking trays with non-stick baking paper.

Sift together the flour, baking powder, baking soda and salt, stir in the chocolate chips and set aside.

Cream the butter, brown sugar and superfine sugar together until light and creamy.

Beat in the vanilla and eggs then fold into the flour mixture until well combined. Mixture will be a little soft and sticky.

Place spoonfuls of cookie dough the size of a large walnut onto a baking tray then insert a wooden stick into the centre of the cookie.

Bake for about 11–12 minutes. Biscuits should not be overcooked and still be a little soft when taken out of the oven.

Cool biscuits completely in the tray before attempting to remove them.

INDEX

First published in 2015 by New Holland Publishers Pty Ltd
London • Sydney • Auckland

The Chandlery Unit 009 50 Westminster Bridge Road London SE1 7QY United Kingdom
1/66 Gibbes Street Chatswood NSW 2067 Australia
5/39 Woodside Ave Northcote, Auckland 0627 New Zealand

www.newhollandpublishers.com

A record of this book is held at the British Library and the National Library of Australia.

ISBN 9781742577470

Managing Director: Fiona Schultz
Project Editor: Holly Willsher
Designer: Andrew Quinlan
Production Director: Olga Dementiev
Printer: Toppan Leefung Printing Limited
10 9 8 7 6 5 4 3 2 1

Keep up with New Holland Publishers on Facebook
www.facebook.com/NewHollandPublishers